Message on a Shoestring

A publicity handbook

Written and
Illustrated by

Chris Radley

A ministry of World Vision

MARC EUROPE

Radley, Christopher
  Message on a shoestring.
  1. Public relations —— Great Britain ——
  Churches   2. Parishes —— Great Britain
  I. Title
  254.4'0941   BV653

  ISBN 0-947697-37-3

MARC Europe is an integral part of World Vision, an international humanitarian organisation. MARC's object is to assist Christian leaders with factual information, surveys, management skills, strategic planning and other tools for evangelism. MARC also publishes and distributes related books on mission, church growth, management, spiritual maturity and other topics.

Copyright © 1986. ISBN 0 947697 37 3.

Typeset in Britain for MARC Europe, Cosmos House, 6 Homesdale Road, Bromley, Kent BR2 9EX by Traditional Typesetters (using OCR), Whitworth Chambers, Northampton; and printed by Richard Clay (The Chaucer Press) Ltd, Bungay, Suffolk.

ACKNOWLEDGEMENTS

Most of the advice here offered is a distillation of my own direct experience and that of many other Christian and secular groups.

Thanks are due to all respondents to the pre-publication survey carried out among church groups in the United Kingdom: they enriched this book as much with the unself-conscious directness of their approach to communications as with their occasional examples of polished end-products. They confirmed *Message on a Shoestring's* mandate to help raise message-making standards without also raising costs. Two such churches in particular deserve mention – St Paul's, Hasland, and St Peter's Shared Church, Chertsey – for producing materials which match the qualities advocated in these pages and for some clear thinking which improved my advice.

MARC Europe's biannual publication *UK Christian Handbook* has been essential reference and MARC'S editor, Liz Gibson, has practised what I preach by firmly cutting my text down to size.

Chris Radley

DEDICATION

For Carole Patricia Hurst Radley

Contents

Introduction

Making the Message

Message on a Shoestring is about ways and means of making clear messages; it is dedicated to the encouragement of rich variety in the expression of Christian ideas and activities. From one Christian tradition to another, from one district to another, opportunities will vary. In the same way, the outworking of the Spirit will vary. What your church group can do in its own individual way is to secure a greater share of public attention and response. This handbook will help you towards that aim by suggesting approaches to planning, to creating and getting your messages to others. The aim is to make your church team objective, not subjective, active, not just reactive.

On a Shoestring

The essence of a good, memorable and motivating message lies in simplicity. Simplicity, though, is not easily attained. Between you and the intended recipient is a route to be plotted, boulders of misunderstanding or distraction to be removed before the connection takes place. To accomplish the journey, commercial agencies spend profligately and, in so doing, confuse the scene with millions of messages coming at the audience through every waking moment. This frenetic activity often results in triviality, where novelty of presentation becomes more important than content. It does, however, have one good effect: most people develop a critical filter that helps them reserve their serious attention for propositions of real, if not 'serious', interest to them.

With a simple message and a clear view of the precise audience you want, it is possible to make publicity on a shoestring. Indeed there are occasions when expensively produced materials can be counterproductive – people finding the glossiness inappropriate to the subject. But inexpensive should not mean inept. There is every justification for unpaid work – none at all for an amateurish end-product. Even uneducated people are sophisticated about selling images, and instinctively equate scruffily-produced materials with inefficiency or untrustworthiness; anything poorly presented will be summarily rejected. For this reason above all others, churches that take satisfaction in spending nothing at all on broadcasting their message should review their motives most critically. If yours is purely a person-to-person ministry, you may have a case for discarding all aids. If this is not so, then to plead lack of cash or human resources simply won't do. This help, if sought, can be found. Having found it, by all means use it most carefully. This book can help.

Message on a Shoestring offers the best of commercial experience as a vehicle for strong, direct publicity. Where type-*writing* is to be used rather than type*setting*, this book offers advice on the layout and the number of words needed to make a leaflet leap to the eye rather than languish in a paper basket. Where you have no budget for media advertising but do have helpers to mobilise, this book offers advice on management.

Quite how and when the Lord may bless the work your team does his name is not the province of this book. What we can do together is to marshal your talents and resources skilfully so as to engage the most opportunities at the wisest cost (which is not the same as saying the *least* cost). There is no blueprint for a series of standardised communications, but the challenge to your team is to think objectively and to discover their gifts fully – as a team, not as a set of maverick individualists. The book does not assume that trained people are available to you; rather it supposes you must do everything with personnel who bring little more than intelligence and enthusiasm.

In Part III you will find a DIY section to help with such designer tasks as the application of dry transfer lettering for headlines, tips for writers approaching readers who are not just a captive audience, as well as advice to others co-operating in specialist tasks.

Quite deliberately this handbook does not set out to offer a ready-reference format. What it does offer is a context for the making of more effective Christian messages.

Getting That Context Right

Anxious to address current church needs, I carried out a postal survey. One thousand churches of different denominations and locations throughout Britain were asked to send, with comment, recent examples of published materials. From their generous response a clearer picture emerges of church groups' needs. It will come as no surprise to hear that cost-consciousness is high and that a sense of helplessness is often apparent, though never a sense of defeat.

This book attempts to address genuine needs while challenging Christian message-makers to greater ambition. Those of the Living Faith must surely choose to breathe more life into their messages.

Part I
Planning

Consider Your Objectives

A healthy church community has two main preoccupations: to sustain the quality of its present life, religious and social, then to extend its action and service. There is no church – however successful in late twentieth century terms – which has no new work to do. For most the tasks are legion, so that it is urgent that they isolate the key challenges. To review them, you might begin by constructing a list of questions, such as:

What is our church's programme for this year, for the next five years?

What are our commitments to external missions, associations, local groups, local churches, local schools? And to internal programmes concerning our congregation's religious/social calendar?

What running costs are estimated over and above those routine items covered by established income sources? What investment is going to be necessary to preserve/improve fabric, equipment and services?

Will major ambitions (a larger or extended church building, for example) create duplication or lack of direction in our short-term activities?

Is the sum of these commitments covered by our established income? If it falls short, by how much? As we examine those commitments, are they all still essential and appropriate to our present and future plans?

Are there other, more pressing candidate commitments already apparent?

How many people are in the family of our church? What is our average attendance to the main services?

Are our active worshippers predominantly male or female? Elderly, middle-aged or young? Is this pattern changing, static? Is it going the way we want it to?

What is our community like? Where do needs lie among the elderly, the shut-ins, the divorced, the spiritually and physically hungry?

If our resources are under-used, how else could we make use of them? If our resources are stretched, what new resources might give us freedom to expand?

If our pastoral commitments are changing (consolidating two parishes into one, for example), how will this affect the factors already mentioned?

What items of communication do we regularly distribute to our constituency? What items are routinely displayed on church premises? What occasional items have we distributed or displayed? (For example, over the past three years?) Were they all necessary, all appropriate, all adequate? Are there glaring gaps in communication?

Has there been a system, a pattern to their planning, production, and distribution, or were they handled randomly? With hindsight, was the planning (or lack of it) productive?

Do these items add up to a 'family' of messages that well expresses our church's concerns, aims and character? Do they fit the present and planned directions of our ministry? Taking the six most essential items from our past output – including everything printed, displayed, broadcast or distributed – which best expresses the real style of our church? Are we using the correct medium of communication in every case? What would we do differently now?

Having examined these aspects of your routine message-making, leaving aside formal church services or elements of religious instruction if you prefer, you should see a picture emerging of the kind of impact you are making on your main membership and neighbourhood audiences. You may perhaps be generally aware of this picture, yet such a review can bring into sharp relief a previously unfocussed impresssion.

Now, before you make a single move towards improving these staple, routine messages, look once more at your wider objectives:

> Are there unreached segments of our community we intend to address?

> Have we a new programme of evangelism in mind? Has its process been thought through?

> Are there local community social/social welfare projects in which our church aims to play a part?

Consider Your Full Programme

See your programme as a whole, as it should be for now and for the future. Once you have examined your resources, it will become plain what range of ambitions your church can truly entertain. Follow through on your examination because it will reveal not only what your commitments are, but exactly which activities comprise your minimum. From that point you can also determine which activities are optional, but which you dearly wish to include in the programme. Obviously, their cost represents the additional funds you need to raise.

A fundraising phase serves not only to get cash, but also to give you a strong sense of which of your volunteers have the makings of a regular team of message-makers. The satisfaction and confidence gained from setting and achieving an income target will carry them over into further challenges. Note that fundraising is discussed on pages 76-83 and the construction of a team capable of good message-making is covered by the section headed Marshal Your Forces on page 21.

Check Your Options

A church group may use an almost infinite number of subjects and formats to convey its messages. Most messages are self-selecting, arising out of routine needs; but others – remember the war cry of the sixties: 'The medium is the message'? – may actually help shape their own physical form. For items concerning the spiritual teaching and worshipping aspects of church life, in Lent, for instance, your own denomination may provide ready-made materials. You may choose to base some stylistic elements of your other message-making on these materials, though this needs to be thoughtfully decided; if their character is austere and you wish to suggest more warmth for your other messages, then you must balance the two so as not to confuse people. If they are exclusive in style and content, useful only for established worshippers, you must view that as a separate audience and set about meeting other needs in other ways.

Here follows a list of typical subjects for message-making, to which you will be able to add others. Check through for any obvious gaps in your programme, bearing in mind that sometimes a single activity may simultaneously satisfy more than one goal.

1 Church Member-based Activities

Special services

Stewardship/pledge payment schemes

Church magazines

Calendar event notifications

Printed prayer materials, seasonal teaching materials

Calls for volunteers

Cash appeals for home church/overseas mission purposes

Joint-church activities

2. Wider Parish Activities

Special services invitations

Newsheets, circulars on activities

Invitations to social events

Invitations to entertainments, lectures, debates

Offers of social/catering services for elderly, infirm, in family trouble

Outings for children, elderly, infirm

Major Christian rallies

Recruitment to clubs for special age/interest groupings

Social problems clinics

Coffee mornings, breakfasts, feasts, fasts and get-togethers

Playgroup crêche, babysitting

3 General Contact Activities

Home visitation programmes

School visitation programmes

Submission of news, views to media and PR for events

Participation in competitions, choral/drama, Bible knowledge etc

Involvement in local cultural festivals, events

Hiring out of church facilities

Social action deputations, protests, petitions

Public speaking

Word-of-mouth contact

Bring-a-friend or neighbour introductory events

Telephone advice/contact schemes

4 Fundraising Activities

Sales of all kinds

Garden parties, fêtes

Sponsored events, covenanting drives

Entertainments

Direct mail, doorstep/street collecting

Media appeals

See also the section headed *Department of Bright Ideas* , (p.83) where some of these activities are examined in detail to stimulate your group into devising its own versions.

Analyse Your Audience

Nothing is more important in the making of effective messages than fully understanding the composition of your audiences – who they are, where they are, what does and does not matter to them – insight without which no real communication takes place. Oddly, this need is often the least considered, and the reasons why they are worth looking at. The main one is – simply – that you probably assume you already know your audience. On the surface it seems obvious that any clergyman knows his patch inside-out, having served it for years and accumulated an understanding of how families and relatives connect, where in the community are the activist elements, what the problems are, what the

Christian/secular composition is, and much else besides. What the pastor has synthesised is a complexity of events now so familiar that he no longer applies analytical thought; yet when he has a message to deliver, it is to this block group that he directs it. The discipline is to work between the general group and the named individual, looking for subgroups defined by their situations and needs. The big, amorphous group encourages a distant form of contact typified by the form of official church calendars. The kind of contact possible at personal level is the perfect model for communicating anything, but it does not work once you step back from the one-to-one meeting. The closest you can get is to identify a *median person* for your project, a capable middle-aged mother of late-teen children or a disenchanted, unemployed young person not long in your parish. Once you see your picture, you are talking directly to the person, you have roughly duplicated the kind of familiarity there is in a personal conversation. And when you write your message with that median person in mind, *what* you say and *how* you say it will strike directly through to people in their respective situations. Never mind that the message is of less importance to peripheral readers, for you will be much closer to your objective of engaging those most likely to respond positively.

In all this, the determinant is always the nature of the message you have in mind. By sharpening the vision of your target, you sharpen your message and inevitably make a crisp impact on a few, rather than a woolly impression on many — as the Christian church often does. (Later, in advice to the writers of messages, p 109-118, the subject of the corporate 'voice' will be discussed.)

An ever-present danger for the Christian communicator is the tendency to take the authoritarian line. 'I bring you this, and you take it. It is good for you, so I need do no more.' All two-way contact is gone. But it is surely our task in both reaching and teaching people to engage first their attention, then their hearts and minds; for unless we identify as closely as possible with them, how can we bring them to us? The dialogue starts where *they* are.

Who Are You Talking To?

Professional advertisers subdivide the masses on behalf of their products, finding their hot chocolate drinkers in one medium and their life assurance prospects in another, having labelled them with considerations of age, sex, occupation, class, social influences, and all the rest of it. Having slotted the larger group into myriad smaller groups (each person appearing in several combinations), they look at such mirages as lifestyles and social aspirations. All this is with the intent of reaching the largest numbers of specific groups through the media they read, listen to or watch – at the cheapest price.

All this labelling goes on, usually, at a national or regional level and is most exacting. Though we may find it unsavoury, we must see that it can be helpful, suitably adapted, in our own work. The professionals present it as a science, but it is in fact common sense, unremittingly applied. What it tells us, at our local level, is to direct our messages to groups we feel we understand, whose circumstances make them most likely to respond. Ultimately it is cheaper, works better, and engages people so strongly that the contact travels beyond the boundaries of one message to allow open, two-way communication.

How can you 'read' the people in your parish without the aid of consumer technology? Start by listing your usual members, subdividing them into groups of your selection, certainly by age, perhaps by occupation, possibly by those who give their time or funds regularly rather than randomly. This is not meant to be an intrusion, but an assessment of individual requirements. Simply begin to line up people's obvious needs and characteristics with your range of objectives. Where they connect, you have a stronger likelihood of pleasing both parties, without wasting money and effort. To these groups can be added names from among occasional worshippers and within the local community. As new contacts are made naturally through church activity, new names may be added.

This mix of the instinctive and the ordered can prove most

efficient. Commercial firms call this approach a database and computerise it, also entering categories in which people are listed according to the amount and frequency of their spending, or by the type of merchandise they consistently prefer. In such a process, the temptation is to exploit, as those firms may care only about one half of the transaction: what they do for the 'client' is only what is essential to keep them 'active' – ie spending. But Christians need not flinch from some of the more direct lessons to be learnt from such analytical care. After all, our perspective is that it is the person who matters, not the resource he represents. (See p. 63 on a church *Who's Who*.) By limiting our analysis to what serves the individual as well as the church, we can easily avoid insensitive behaviour.

Privacy and confidentiality must be strictly observed particularly in the case of financial information. Note that, apart from the ethical considerations involved with collecting information, there are legal constraints. If you wish to store personal information in any machine-readable format (ie on a computer or word processor), you must register officially with the Data Protection Registrar (Springfield House, Water Lane, Wilmslow, Cheshire SK9 5AX) the purpose of your storing the data, the type of information stored and its source, and the persons to whom you will disclose the data.

The real value of such an index, kept fully up-to-date with addresses and other information, begins to show after perhaps a year or two of careful attention to detail and some trial runs, when the various groups of the main list are tested. You will then see if your judgements about the ideal respondents for a particular appeal or other message were proved right in action. Apart from that, the index and the lists you draw from it should stop you from asking the same generous few too often; it may help identify the helper who will help only when asked long in advance or, by contrast, the person who likes a challenge and responds better when some urgency is involved. It should help you to understand what kinds of people come to various events, and later on, when reading the information becomes second nature, you will know who is or is not ready to be challenged to greater involvement.

Wider Still, Yet Wider

Beyond this index – this 'map' of your church community – there is another kind of map: one that notes all the public media that overlap the parish. Each local newspaper or freesheet, each local radio station has a defined circulation area. You should know what influence each has in your parish, how well each is thought of by your community. Newsagents will tell you how many copies are ordered, and the media can usually provide some information on audience figures – some even specifying precisely which ages or types of people predominate. It will help you to assess them as advertising media should you ever have the cause or the funds to buy space but, more usefully, will tell you which are worth supplying with facts, stories, interviews or articles about your church activities.

A Little Research Goes a Long Way

With your index 'map' and your media 'map', making decisions about audiences becomes easier. Where neither the facts nor your local experience can illuminate, don't be shy about asking people. If you are considering a big effort for a scheme reaching out into the wider local area, check its chances first, by all means.

Asking people isn't difficult; *what* you ask them is difficult. If you ask a group of young RAF officers in their mess which daily newspapers they read, they will name all the so-called 'serious' papers; if you look around you, you will see abundant evidence that the popular reading is more of a tabloid shape. In short, they are giving you the answer they think you want, or the answer that reflects best on them. For this reason, sending a few people a postal questionnaire hoping to get a batch of honest answers to straightforward questions is not going to work unless a market research expert

16

has put the thing together. For your purposes, consider the method used by some political canvassers. They put questionnaires through letter-boxes one evening, asking the family to complete them in time for collection the following evening. The questions are not personal, but involve opinions about the state of the neighbourhood. When the canvassers call back the next day, not many people have completed the sheets, but they are not apprehensive about the matter and will happily give answers to all the questions as the interviewers read them out. The canvassers are looking for information which can lead them to take helpful action and thus win some approval; they are also hoping to build familiarity. For your own church purposes, though the aims and motives may be different, the process can be rewarding.

Are Your Members Representative?

It is important that you compare statistically the composition of your main membership with that of the community around you. If it differs in some clear way – by age or background, say – then you need to understand why. You need to know whether this is a fixed or changing position and to draw from it conclusions leading to action. It is only by such comparisons that a church can remain in a state of healthy growth – a lesson underlined by the series of census exercises in England, Wales and Scotland by MARC Europe, where the denominations themselves have been shown statistically what has not always been apparent to them 'from close up'. For you at the more modest level, knowledge is also strength.

By knowing your audiences, you know where the opportunities are, what is missing from your communications materials, and how to put it right. How much better than to live on vague assumptions which can only encourage inactivity or defensiveness.

Know Your Channels

As well as the homework your group does on its audiences,

encourage the group to review the channels of communication available. Later you will evaluate their usefulness as you measure them against your programme of building relationships and making messages. Depending on those plans, you will arrive at a 'media mix' exactly right for your church. Of course, it may be that everything you do will be run off on your own duplicating machine and distributed by hand; it is likely, though, that a range of media will be used to cover everything in a busy church year. Whatever the pattern used, think of the means by which your message reaches the audience.

A squad of church newsletter distributors is a channel, as is the organiser of speakers for a local social club, or the features editor of the local paper.

From the list of channels given below – to which you will be able to add others once your team gives it some thought – identify those which could serve your message-making. Trace the names, telephone numbers and addresses of the contact people for those channels. Be sure to meet them and to understand their interests and professional needs.

1 Published Channels	2 Display Channels
Regional/local press	Newsagents cards
Freesheets (door drop)	Fly-posting where allowed
Post Office special delivery services	Railway station posters
County/local magazines	
Religious press	Church notice boards
	High Street store windows, including banks, building societies
News sheets of local societies/organisations	Portable exhibition stands for church, schools, event and in store display, etc, perhaps donated
Local public radio, hospital radio	Countertop leaflet dispensers for friendly retailers
Regional TV, later cable and satellite TV	Collection boxes
Direct mail	Sandwich boards

Local traders' catalogues (piggyback)

Other local church publications

Banners, buttons, badges and on-clothing messages

Travelling displays in vans or floats

Sponsored event ephemera

The outsides of cars, vans and public transport

Bus stop 'shell' posters, billboard sites, house windows

3 Personal Editorial Channels

Local/regional journalists

Religious media journalists

Local radio/TV producers

Editors of club or school news letters, college magazines, local firms' house news sheets

Contributors to any of the above

4 Grassroots Channels

Talks for groups, schools

Shows for groups, schools

Recorded answerphone messages

Hand-delivered messages, from handwritten notes to leaflets – religious, social and fundraising

Sales, fairs, public events of all kinds where additional messages may be added

Fundraising events

Good-neighbour activities

Inter-church links

Church club groups

Word-of-mouth campaigns

Contacts with local hospitals, nursing homes, retirement complexes

Contact with local government

Almost any channel to the public in your area can carry one of your messages. Depending on the persuasive powers of your team, such opportunities may be costly, cheap or free. Do not suppose that your audience will frown on such initiative-taking; it is the content and character of what you do that matter to them; they'll almost certainly be impressed by your church's energy and imagination in reaching them via some unexpected route.

On page 21, under the heading *Marshal Your Forces*, advice is offered on the dividing of responsibilities within your church group. The access to channels for the elements of your campaign can be shared by those who are not previously initiated in such skills, but who will rapidly become so. Your team can develop a blend of messages and methods unique to your church. You'll have to nurse it along, avoid self-indulgence on the part of 'creative' team members and undue caution on the part of traditionalists, but you will arrive at a true representation instantly identifiable by your audiences as *yours*. Large commercial organisations spend tens of thousands for the same result, calling it 'corporate identity'. But then, theirs may incorporate a certain amount of fiction, while yours does not.

Deal with People, Not Experts

Sitting at the entrance to each channel is a person preoccupied with his own problems. Your access is largely dependent on this person, so you must make personal contact. The communications industry thinks in terms of public relations or media relations; but you should see them as personal relations, for at that level only will your relatively small demands get noticed and granted access. Despite the expectations, many are willing to help and respond to well presented materials, sensitively offered. Busy social club organisers and local radio producers can find time to help. Co-operation depends on your attitude, for nobody wants to feel like a lever to be pulled. Church people above all others need to regard such contacts as friends travelling the same road.

Whether your contact is a local newsagent (whose delivery-boys you aim to have plant your message through letterboxes along with the newspapers), or a local radio programme producer (who just might regard your message as a reasonable expression of her station's statutory duty to broadcast 'community content' subjects), do get to know them, their roles and their needs as people. Once their needs and yours coincide, the channel is open.

Get to know also the costs, the deadlines, the contact details and the mechanical requirements of each channel. Is it the first Monday of the month by which time you must deliver text to the county magazine, or is it on a fixed date? Do they want complete artwork, or will they assemble it for you? And whose name do you write on the envelope?

Watch out for what other communicators do; new channels opening all the time, with new ways to use them. What about the person who first thought of releasing clouds of lighter-than-air balloons with messages tied to them and competition prizes for the furthest flight? That is typical of ideas that are un-copyrightable.

In particular, seek channels unique to your locality. If you happen to have a town crier, use him. If you have local historic traditions, think of them as channels. The opportunities are many.

Do not fret at lack of funds, for it is not always a drawback: it concentrates minds wonderfully, releasing energy and imagination, and binds your team together as you meet and overcome difficulties.

Marshal Your Forces

Who made the messages you currently use? Do you have a group with this responsibility? Or just one or two people struggling with it? Are things merely coped with, or are they smoothly prepared when deadlines begin to press? It is usual to discover that, apart from the items on the regular calendar of activities, people attend and react to most things only as they arise; frequently, they have no time to reflect on the overall direction of the work. Even more commonly, one person does it all himself . . . and he is the clergyman.

In your church's resolve to challenge the local community to witness and participation, this One Man Band approach is

21

not the answer. However capable that person is, or however little sleep he may need, his not having the time to think through opportunities for message-making undercuts all the value of his knowledge of the parish and the exercise of his gifts. Counsel for the defence of the clergyman might here say, 'But how can this hard-pressed man make the space to recruit other capable helpers?' To this one must reply, 'Make the time. It is so important that your church gets ahead of the pressures that it would be a small sacrifice indeed to cut out of the schedule for just one month say an edition of the church magazine.' The only other argument (apart from claiming the parish is inhabited entirely by over-eighties) is the one about the fear of creating more committees. This is worth a serious answer. No clergyman could possibly want more all-talk, no-action groups draining the church's energy. His defence counsel might reasonably quote the well-known saying 'A camel is just a horse designed by a committee.' One response to that is Ambrose Bierce's comment: 'Only Christians and camels receive their burden kneeling.' Let's be Christians, not camels – active, not passive.

If you do not already have a team of message-makers for your church, then, this is the ideal time to recruit one, or to top up the numbers. And if you do have such a team, don't be exclusive; involve some new people anyway.

The danger of futile committees is resolved when you decide to recruit a team of doers, not a committee of super-visors. Gather a group of women and men who wish to do something positive, and who share a proper aversion to the kind of committee discussion which can devote half-an-hour to the one and true price of jam tarts for the Summer Fair. You do not need a battery of trained writers, artists or printers; it is their attitude that matters. Where high skills are available to you, they must, if possible, be employed, but motivation and intelligence are quite sufficient raw materials for you to be working with. This handbook proceeds from the assumption that ready-made skills are not available to you.

22

Before the 'how to do it', then, let us deal with the 'who to do it'. First, one more word about skill. Do not fall into the trap of accepting that, simply because someone may have an aptitude or hobby of a general artistic nature, he should automatically become your group's designer; nor, even though one of your number once read Anglo-Saxon, she should be handed the responsibility for writing. Application and commitment are by far the more important attributes – so much so that, as the book outlines each of the tasks for any team, it stresses personal qualities far more than technical skills.

Recruiting Practical People

In recruiting any team member, the objective must be to help a person gain expertise in his role, while ensuring that he is sufficiently unpossessive of the knowledge to share it freely with others. The standard has to be the effectiveness of the end-product, though the work itself should also be rewarding. The decorative qualities of a design do not matter as much as its impact on a chosen audience; it is not the literary purity of the words that must be pre-eminent, but their ability to convince. (This is not a plea for bad grammar!).

Gather your 'doers', then, in the light of the roles to be described, looking always for a blend. You need a strong team capable of producing anything from a Stewardship Campaign to a Sponsored Hop, from a Bring & Buy leaflet to a Day of Prayer programme. Each function suggested here is a distillation of much church group watching, along with observation of secular groups making messages for a variety of purposes. Function by function, this book reviews the tasks; once you are convinced of their value to your church, some mental screening will be in order. It is better to invite people to take on particular tasks than to allow a democratic process to take place. There will almost certainly be more roles to fill than obvious candidates, so it is unlikely that someone keen is going to be left out.

To keep things simple, the eight basic roles or functions have been given titles; these you will be most unlikely to use in reality, but they serve to focus the information. Recognising that not all church groups will be able to muster eight capable enthusiasts, you will find at the end of this section a variety of permutations of role so that all can be done, even when the group is down to four. Conversely, should you be overwhelmed by volunteers, do not expand the roles to engage more people; rather set up alternates for each function so that the skills may be spread without confusion. By all means develop task teams beyond the main group and let them handle leaflet delivery, money collection, telephone contact and so on. Be sure to avoid a debating society.

The arbitrary team labels used here are: Leader, Cashier, Forager, Fixer, Chaser, Writer, Designer and Reporter. We offer no recipe for what age, sex or occupation may best suit each role, except to say that a good mixture will work best. The gender of pronouns used is in no way prescriptive!

Be advised not to drop this workload into the laps of some existing committee. Even if they are in the end the best people to do the work, first open your options. You owe it to hitherto uninvolved people to get this chance to serve and find fulfilment.

The Leader

Should the religious leader automatically became the message-makers' leader? As the clergyman usually takes the first steps in this, he alone must resolve the issue. He will be inclined to answer 'yes'. After all, he is trained in a vocation at the very centre of which is communication. Yet is he the logical choice here? And is a decisive parson the same as a decisive person? A quietly decisive person will, in fact, prove more effective than a charismatic one. Whoever is selected will need to be centrally involved with the life of the church and have sufficient vision to realise the rich variety of message-making opportunities. Thus a clergyman is likely to have only two reasons for not commandeering the role of Leader. One is that he may feel overstretched in his pastoral duties; the other is that some other candidate of quality leaps immediately to mind. But this puts pressure on him. Knowing that his wishes are likely to be unopposed, is he right to deny some other, possibly more able organiser the Leader role?

The Leader in particular gains from his continual involvement, just as the entire team gains stability from dealing with one person over a period. Do not therefore make someone Leader who offers brilliance as a substitute for reliable involvement.

There are as many ways to lead as there are leaders – since of course the performance springs from the natural qualities of the person – yet there are some ground rules to follow. At the start of any new project the Leader asks for opinions and listens thoughtfully to them; he seeks consensus but is not bound by it. When the project is active he kindly but firmly declines unproductive comment. A readiness to referee: to decide 'yes' or 'no' and an aversion to the word 'perhaps' is helpful, as indecision encourages argument. Adults of any real character dislike being 'managed', much preferring a challenge to action which they can positively accept and thus identify with. Volunteers can be guided into businesslike ways as long as there is enjoyment also present in the process.

Someone with a good grip of housekeeping might do such organising well; the Leader's role can be every bit as much a woman's as a man's job. Just make sure the person can delegate!

Nothing the Leader does is more important than to keep everybody's spirits high. He asks for loyalty only in God's service and reinforces team spirit through regular prayer, however unstructured. He is, in fact, a Barnabas – a son of encouragement – and could even consider providing the team with a biblical framework for its actions, a unifying thread.

Having agreed the aims and production plan for a project, and having agreed the budget, the Leader remains available to make decisions and give guidance, but should primarily be concerned with wider, longer-range plans. Every current action must to some extent affect the pace and direction of longer-term objectives, and it is the Leader's task to maintain a workable vision. Powerful communications can take on a life of their own and distort intentions; poor work can sink the best-laid plans. Someone has to pay attention all the time.

The Leader should set the objectives down on paper, along with the strategy, the budget allocations and the time-plan. The system for approving solutions to problems should be kept simple, ideally involving only the Leader's signature. (Running this system is a role for the Chaser.)

At the conclusion of a project, by all means gather the team to review the experience. Encourage, do not hold a post mortem. Take care to say, 'Next time we'll increase the type-size,' rather than 'The typesize was too small.' People are tender at times like these. Get the specialists to evaluate their own contributions, for they will usually be more merciless to themselves than any outsider could. Use such meetings as bridges to the next project, and be sure that people leave feeling buoyant.

It is for the Leader to equalise pressures, watching with the

Chaser (who gets things out on time), to ensure no one person feels put-upon. This is one opportunity for the Leader to pitch in and help relieve the pressure. It is for the Leader to maintain contact with team members between projects, thanking them for their service. Make no attempt to run an unbroken programme of messages, since your people have private and working lives to fit in somewhere and will work better when there is 'light and shade' to the church involvement! Volunteers work best in bursts of energy broken by periods of no demand at all. The Leader must watch for this as he must also watch for signs of weariness, ready to refresh individuals by a change of responsibility should the signs show.

The Cashier

The difference between the Treasurer and the Cashier roles is important to your group. It may prove expedient for the Treasurer of your church to perform this sub-function for the message-making group. It would be better to have someone who, while reporting back to the official officer, sees the handling of money not as a formal process, but as a pragmatic one. The Cashier has to be accessible in a way the Treasurer need not be. This suggests some special character-istics, the first of which is in the attitude to money. Either despite or because people are intensely money-conscious these days, you may encounter considerable un-willingness to handle it. Professional accountants can be forgiven if they are unwilling to do in the evenings what they do all day; don't press them: their comfort in dealing with large sums may be inappropriate to your 'shoestring' operation. Find someone who is numerate, certainly, but with an open attitude to the handling of scarce resources. Someone with a trading background could be best of all.

At one South London church, the 'volunteer' was proving reluctant. He was 20, unwaged and understandably low in self-confidence. To him, money was an elusive commodity, to be treated with respect, but no more. The Cashier's job looked to him like a frontier post marking the divide between usefulness and uselessness. It took him a year of handling the stuff for the church team, earning thanks rather than cash for his efforts, before he really settled to the role. He knows what money costs and won't have it wasted.

While your Cashier must record all transactions, the role is more than that, perhaps something akin to an expedition's quartermaster, working with the Leader, the Forager and the Fixer in adapting to changing circumstances within an established budget.

As each project starts, the Cashier must know to the penny what money has been allocated. She prepares the cheques for the Treasurer to issue; she carries a petty cash float for small, out-of-pocket costs and a file for the running projects in which she tracks everything from estimates to invoices. A non-professional can bring one useful attitude to bear: she can regard a budget as something which should be spent, but not overspent. Professionals almost instinctively act as defenders of the funds, delaying payment and pressing cuts. Your team should make and stick to a budget in order to learn how best to judge things for the future. The Cashier must play defender of the funds when the group is in initial discussion about its use across many projects, after that using it in such a way that other team members do not need to feel guilty when asking for cash.

The Cashier should take a positive attitude also to out-of-pocket expenses. She should discourage the tendency to spend without reclaiming. The attitude must be 'If you wish to make a donation, put it in the church collection box.' The thinking here is practical on two levels: If the Cashier is not getting a full picture of outgoings, then the basis for future budget is false; and if not everyone is collecting such expenses, then those on slender means will be put in an awkward position and may be discouraged from helping.

When considering your candidates for Cashier, plan that role as part of the subgroup comprising Cashier, Forager and Fixer, who will work closely on many tasks. Their personalities need to blend well.

28

The Forager

Foraging is a time-honoured calling. The Disciples did it; the Children of Israel in their wanderings did it. Just as armies march on their stomachs, so must church groups proceed on a shoestring. Modern communications are mass-market affairs, building the public's expectations ever higher. Cost-cutting somehow succeeds only when the scale of operations is big, whereas those with small budgets and small production runs stand at a disadvantage. Your group must therefore decide that paying market rate for anything must be only as a reluctant last resort. One of you must be so convinced that the local sources and suppliers will be persuaded to surrender a part at least of their cherished profits, facilities, resources or belongings. Your Forager can do this even more easily than you might suppose.

Forager candidates reveal themselves by their very passage through life, never taking 'no' for an answer and losing no popularity over it. They are the lateral thinkers, the optimists, the incorrigibles. You will have at least one in your church. Gender and occupation should not matter, but age may be critical. Too young and the authority to back up the unreasonable demands may not seem real, too old and the lack of physical energy may limit him.

A natural Forager never feels he is taking a liberty when asking for help. One such clear-headed person from Diss explained, 'Not everybody has the wonderful opportunity to give of himself, but there is nothing to stop him giving of his worldly goods!' This perception leaves no member of the congregation, no neighbour, no contact – no stranger, even – safe. And those who have no support to offer can always introduce your Forager to others who have.

Has all this given you a picture of the Forager as dragon? Not so. The successful Forager is disarmingly and genuinely gentle. He uses no bullying, harassment or arm-twisting. The slightest disinclination to help should be responded to with a 'thank-you' and a departure, followed by another call on another day with a different request. Painlessly, this encourages people to be ready to give freely, eventually to offer before they are asked. The Forager takes literally the general acceptance of the notion that it is better to give than to receive and is proved right time after time as he sees people who once helped reluctantly, now helping willingly, discovering that they are receiving.

What, then, needs to be foraged? The Forager seeks four main types of help: *money or gifts* which can be converted into cash by resale at church events; *offers of facilities* such as venues, transport or printing services free or at cost; *offers of materials* for stationery, printing, exhibitions or events; *offers of skilled help* of all kinds. There is another hold-all category you might add: *windfalls* – an offer that comes through when you haven't been asking, sometimes hard to fit into your programme, but impossible to refuse – such things as Marks & Spencer's food department offering you all its fresh but unsold perishables late Saturday afternoon!

The skilled Forager has two agenda always in mind, the first being the general order of the year's programme, so that he can readily accept anything of potential value when offered; the second being an awareness of precise and immediate needs, not accepting inappropriate gifts. For active projects the foraging has to be precise if it is not to work against clear provision already made. The story of a Norfolk church group illustrates the danger: Their Forager was offered the loan of a portable exhibition stand by a local manufacturer. The church had been working with a local school on a Food for Africa show, this to be erected in the church lobby for a week's display, proceeds to a well-known charity. Three days before opening, the manufacturer duly dismantled his portable stand from a trade fair and had it sent to the church. About that time the artistic product of the classes of sevens-to-elevens arrived in assorted sizes of paper, all illustrating the African famine. It took six people to assemble the stand into the only configuration that would fit the lobby: a cramped three-quarter circle. The stand's lighting was intensely bright but had to be used since the stand was blocking the normal lobby lighting. The light hurt people's eyes and the display created congestion. The panels were placed too high for the children's work to be seen without dazzle from the lights. The next electricity bill also made a dent in the money collected. When you forage, forage to a plan.

The Fixer

When you have considered all the roles here described you may conclude that, as you have a Forager, you may not need a Fixer. Only if your planned programme is extremely modest or your available audience small in number and already well-attended to, might this be true. If you can, have a Fixer because she performs many money-saving tasks.

The Fixer does the booking and the buying for your group. She sees to it that materials offered (or foraged) are collected and, where necessary, safely returned. The Fixer becomes a walking reference for comparative prices, understands print processes and other such technicalities as where to get audio tapes copied, or 35mm slides, or photoprints. Responsibility for timely assembly and storage of everything from cardboard displays to carnival floats, from the erection of canvas marquees to direct mail collation and delivery – all will be hers. She will recruit a squad of leaflet deliverers (leafleteers) and know how to mobilise them quickly.

A recently retired person can very well suit this role, particularly if she has a car and a lot of energy. Being retired, she will have no need to compress visits to instant print shops or other suppliers into lunch hours or weekends. The quest for the perfect price (ie free) need not then be fitted-in between the dropping-off and collecting of children. She has the time, the patience and the experience to buy cannily, and should be allowed car and telephone expenses.

Choose someone who takes pride in being well-organised, one who actually likes recording detail and filing information. In a short while a considerable body of practical knowledge will be assembled, material which is the property of the team and must not be stored only in the Fixer's head. Even Fixers

31

take holidays or get ill, so her experience should be recorded in such a way that others have no difficulty picking up a task at any stage.

Ask your Fixer to maintain your group's list of names, addresses and telephone numbers, if possible including people's business numbers also, adding clear instructions as to which times are convenient to make contact. Each team member needs that list; it can be one of the Chaser's tasks to ensure that everybody holds the latest edition. If the Chaser is to take on this job, he might care to use the reverse of the list to give the latest timings for the various stages of current projects. As you will probably hold complete group meetings only seldom, this item serves as a newsheet. In all questions of who does what, the Leader decides.

Inevitably, you will find a certain overlap between roles, and this can be encouraged as long as there is no danger of muddle. The Fixer in the normal course of duties will certainly bump into opportunities to forage, just as any of the others may get chances to secure good bookings or cheap materials. Always refer such decisions to the specialist with that particular responsibility. The Fixer will see bargains in her rounds of suppliers and must be permitted to make decisions without referring back, within understood cash limits. If she is offered, say, a bulk quantity of paper for printing, she will consult with the Designer to be sure it suits the 'look' required and the Cashier to check that making such an investment makes sense in the long run. The Leader arbitrates.

If the group is ambitious, storage is going to be your Fixer's main obsession. She is going to have to be a tiger about this as churches are always centres for a multiplicity of events, run by people not responsible for each other's equipment and often not related otherwise to the church. Items stored by the message-makers must be safe from the foragings of others. At a spring bazaar run by an over-sixties group near Brighton, for instance, over 200 greenhouse-grown potted plants were beautifully wrapped for customers in A2-size *posters* put aside by a fundraising group the previous week. These were preprinted sheets carrying only the church name and symbol, all ready for later overprinting. Your Fixer has to fix it so that such things cannot happen!

The Fixer needs to work closely with the Designer. As you will most likely choose a Designer who has no formal training, the Fixer has to defend against errors – understandable errors – in technique; the preparation of artwork for reproduction is something that has to be the right size and geometrically 'square' – ie corners at right-angles. The Fixer must secure the correct information and help the Designer satisfy its demands.

The Chaser

Here again you have some options should your team be small in numbers and your programme modest: Your Cashier could combine the two roles; or the roles of Fixer and Chaser may be one person's. When doubling-up in this way, let the quality of the person be the deciding factor. Certainly the Cashier/Chaser combination will work well enough if you're confident your colleagues will be tolerant when the same person both quizzes them on expenditure *and* goads them into action! The Fixer/Chaser doubling-up demands someone with the rare combination of energy and spare time. Here we shall proceed as if you are to appoint a solo Chaser.

A Chaser is in charge of time. Working closely with the Leader and Fixer, he has to 'lock on' to the established timetable and permit no bending of it whatsoever. He must also plan each production stage, whether it concerns printing or Marbles Marathons; all along the way the timetable charts named persons and fixed objectives – within a time limit. If conditions or people's commitments change, as they invariably will, he works out a new timetable with the Leader and chases that instead, having first warned every team-member involved how he or she is affected.

As to what kind of person best suits this role, here you have considerable latitude. It is tempting to put in a strong, authoritative person, but you don't want someone straining relationships, however efficient he may be. Nor do you want someone inflexible! Equally tempting is to choose the most liked or the most respected person, but this step could do much for relationships and very little for deadlines. The best candidate may be the least obvious. Think, which of your regular, active members is the one who routinely remembers the small details others miss?

While no serious suggestion is made here for the use of these roles as remedial or therapeutic opportunities, there is value in giving a job to someone who needs a challenge to discover or confirm his self-worth. A Carlisle church's Chaser had been, by his own admission, the least time-conscious or orderly person in the parish. The taking on of the task had revolutionised his attitude, while he retained his tolerance of ordinary human frailties in others when they forgot a meeting or went on holiday without telling him.

Certainly the most vital of the Chaser's jobs is seeing that the pressure of lateness – when minor deadlines over-run – does not roll down the line of specialist tasks and squash the poor soul at the end. If the folks at the start of the project, well away as they are from the final, unbudgable deadline, relax and take a day or two over their allotted period, the Designer suffers and has to make quite unnecessary sacrifices to correct such carelessness. The Fixer also suffers, having to placate her printer and reorganise her leafleteers. For such reasons, the Chaser always chases in advance of a date, anticipating snags, sensing when someone is off-colour or hard-pressed. The Chaser learns to prompt people to articulate their feelings before they are tense about them and is responsible for drawing on the Leader's help early.

Some church groups use the person in this kind of role rather as a repertory company might use a deputy stage manager – as a stand-in for several parts. So, if you have a good generalist in your ranks, perhaps he is your Chaser.

The Writer

It is almost certain that if the clergyman in your church

group does not take on the role of Leader, he will be the Writer. As in most instances the person assembling the team and the clergyman will be one and the same, the remainder of the team is not really in a position to dispute this piece of auto-casting. In some ways this is the easier decision, for all clergy, in their various forms of training for ordination, are made comfortable with language and the ways of communicating the Christian message. For some there will be a desire to be both Writer and Leader. Do not be tempted. You will not have the time to do both well and may undermine the team's confidence.

Of all the skills needed for your team, writing is perhaps the hardest. The difficulty is that everyone – more or less – can write from the age of seven or so, and those who use the written word as a central feature of their professional lives become accomplished in their particular field. Yet such specialised applications of written language can be less than useful in making messages for church growth purposes. This narrow perspective, however, obviously also afflicts many clergymen who are trained to transmit the timeless truths of one faith. A pastor is used to his spiritual tradition, used to audiences defined by spiritual needs. Meanwhile the audience is hearing or reading him from its own limited perspective based on childhood conditioning; this applies both to those who are brought up inside the church family and to those who see themselves outside it.

These limits and expectations create in the audiences ready-made responses to known forms of Christian message. Meeting these conditions is essential and terribly demanding for the Writer, and high skills are needed if the Writer is to break through the audience's habit of not really hearing the message because the form has become a comfort to some and a barrier to others. Even though a clergyman has let light into lives through formal preaching and teaching, he has not necessarily discovered the way to make less directly religious messages work; the thread of connection he wants to estab-lish in this type of message making is not salvation but

35

something more commonplace.

This is hard for an ordained church leader to accept, but for his influence to reach out to the far edges of his community – religiously, not geographically – it must meet people where they happen to be and, having arrived, must speak in a language they can *hear*. This means there is room for neither the 'churchified' tone, nor the jolly, patronising tone often adopted out of sheer inability to bridge what seems like a huge divide.

Writing which truly communicates across the variety of topics that comprise any growing church's messages requires a consistency of tone or 'voice'. Directly religious elements must carry authority, yet be handled in such a way as to be accessible to others concerned with more visible, tangible activities. Each message, by its design and its written style, should be clearly related to the whole family of messages from your church; as in any family, no two members are likely to be exactly alike, yet will seem – literally – *familiar* to the world at large.

These observations apply just as much to communicators working in specialised industries or fields of practice. An 'in-language' emerges, riddled with jargon, mysterious abbreviations and references clear only to the initiated. Both consciously and unconsciously exclusivity builds up. When commercial firms do this as they address their less technically immersed customers or clients, they employ advertising agents who can make a clear transmission of the essential message. When you look at professionals to whom direct publicity is forbidden – lawyers and doctors who may not therefore employ such 'translators' – the writing is necessarily done by the professionals themselves. It is almost always awful, trapped with the technicalities and mannerisms of an exclusive club. You, the reader, are outside the charmed circle and at a disadvantage. The Church is not innocent in this, as many denominational sub-languages exist, so readily distinguishable that Christians can place many of the labels with ease. To those as yet outside our circle these sub-languages blur into one largely inaccessible church language.

Your Writer, whether or not he is also the clergyman, must work against exclusivity by thinking through the mind of the intended recipient, always asking, 'Is this intelligible; is this daunting; does the word choice block understanding?' There is no surer corrective – provided that the Writer has built up a first hand contact with the actual groups of people his messages are for. This is not merely a matter of education. People do not fail to comprehend messages solely because the syntax defeats them; more often something in the presentation suggests it doesn't concern them, that it is a message for somebody else. As the Writer holds an image in mind of the typical reader, somehow the jargon and unhelpful idioms identify themselves as if lit by neon.

Your Writer must to be ready to originate messages as well as to edit texts prepared by someone else. Original writing will be needed for most projects – from long leaflet passages to short slogans for notice boards, from compact, informative passages to persuasive texts in direct mail letters.

The editing function comes from the many minor written items other team members produce, of which there will be a great variety: refreshments tickets, sponsor-participation forms, directional maps to events – not literary pieces, but necessary. When the text has been roughly drafted by a team colleague, the Writer polishes up clarity and the grammar, cuts extra words or adds more material to fit the space available, double-checks for accuracy and ensures it conforms to the general style developed for the church. (See pp 109-118.)

One cautionary note: Disputes over phrasing can bring almost any two ordinarily passive, agreeable human beings into edgy confrontation. It may be something to do with the territorial imperative, and certainly it involves pride. For the clergyman doubling as Writer it demands a particular degree of care not to unduly dominate such exchanges; for the clergyman acting as Leader and in discussion with the Writer, even greater circumspection is essential.

Take special pains to establish a generous working relationship between the Writer and Designer. After the other team members have assembled the facts and the requirements, these two must deliver the goods. Just as the Writer needs to be generous in the matter of the 'ownership' of the words, so she must make room for the visual presentation of those words. A reader stops to read the message because of the marriage of these two skills. The visual consideration in some messages is more critical than the wording, with one pictorial image expressing a meaning instantaneously. At other times, the subject may be so serious that illustrations become intrusive. So in deciding which should lead and which should follow – or, rarely achieved but most desirable, how they may work in perfect balance – an attitude of give-and-take should be your working method. It is the Writer who usually gets first opportunity to consider the project and who can be tempted to button up all the decisions before the Designer can get into the discussion. The Designer will soon realise that her task is going to involve hours of artwork preparation; she may not challenge the Writer's preemptive behaviour, preferring to avoid further delays. But this makes for a mechanical solution, losing your team the opportunity of a message which 'lives'; it also relegates the Designer to hack. Let your Writer be generous in open discussion of every project, thinking objectively. Such objectivity is difficult to achieve, obscured by the modern cult of individualism and the great difficulty of keeping corrosive pride in self-expression out of the process. To subordinate personal pride to the relative anonymity of a team production will be a hard test for some strong wills but – most important – an encouragement to other less strong personalities.

Unfortunately, time is most likely to be lost at the writing stage in any schedule; so the Chaser must ensure that before the Writer is set loose upon the solution, all facts are gathered.

The wise Chaser will have built in adequate margin for error at this stage.

The Designer

Time bears heavily upon this function, and there is seldom enough. This, at one fell stroke does away with romantic ideas about the value of an artistic temperament! You can't afford one. The Designer needs a steady temperament and a practical approach.

Do not suppose that someone who is a potter, a basket weaver or a flower arranger is more qualified to cope with the Designer task than someone else who, while having no obvious creative skills, has enthusiasm and intelligence. You are not looking to produce high art, just strong, simply presented materials able to convey your message in attention-getting and convincing style.

The Chaser can represent both friend and foe to the Designer: friend when he keeps everyone else in the early stages up to schedule, foe when he starts to bring pressure on behalf of the Fixer and her printing timetable. Chasers soon learn to apply positive discrimination here, concentrating on keeping all earlier functions up to or ahead of time. This is wise because nothing looks quite so limp as a hurried design, which – after all – is the tangible end result of everyone else's efforts. There is no disgrace if it is less than beautiful; there is if it is less than clear.

To recruit a logical, resourceful person with adequate visual taste, one who learns fast, likes a challenge and will cooperate, first think of her as one half of a team with the Writer you have selected. Having so selected, encourage your Designer to discard any idea that she is merely a function along a conveyor-belt. The Designer aims for a consensus idea, which is altogether more positive than to make real a compromise. This distinction will become obvious in practice, for a consensus idea allows room for interpretation by the Writer/Designer team, often turning out a much more direct and simple design than had been been expected. Compromise solutions tend to get more complex, So if you have space for only one cryptic message over their kitchen tables, make it this: ONE MAIN CONCEPT FOR ONE MESSAGE. If you have more than one concept or idea, unless the others flow in a natural, sequential way from the first and do not cloud it, then save those ideas for some other message. Put more than one powerful idea or injunction into your message and you divide the reader's attention and lose him. No other single weakness so immediately distinguishes amateur from professional design.

The Designer is at the fulcrum of any project. Before the design stage is the time when all possibilities remain alive, beyond it only the utterly practical ones survive. The balance has to be perfect. She will learn not to accept too many words, too many half-resolved ideas or too few hours left in which to make sense of it all. Not to behave firmly here is to suggest that the Designer has a victim mentality, guaranteeing a miserable time personally and a poor result for the group's labours.

The effective Designer learns to take a hand in the formative process, insisting on a place in the planning, talking through all options with the Writer and Leader well before the Writer has done his work and so feels obliged to defend his words against truncation or undue stress, and before the Leader has approved the basic approach. The good Designer is concerned with the essential impact of a message, wanting it to secure attention, to be read and remembered and to achieve a result – a response. So shaping the presentation of a message is more than the provision of decoration. If you have people with drawing or decorative skills, use them on a commission basis. They will usually prefer this kind of contribution rather than full design.

In asserting herself to this extent, the Designer must not tip the balance with an attitude of domination, demanding too many sacrifices of the Writer in the name of the deadline. The Leader needs to be ready to make adjustments. In any Christian group there are always present the contrary inclinations towards self-sacrifice or passionate assertion. The first makes for lifeless messages, the other for confusion. Remind all concerned that if there is no pleasure in the making of the message, there'll be precious little in the reading of it.

It may help here to list the Designer's principal tasks. More detail will be added later on, pages 122-155.

★ Participate in creative planning, thinking about the way your group could best present the message visually.

★ Talk through the balance of words and pictures or display with the Writer.

★ Understand the demands of the methods to be used, so that artwork can be correctly prepared in conjunction with the Fixer.

★ Develop the skill or find a professional adviser (probably a printer) to help you calculate how many words will fit into a given area on the artwork without being cramped into too small a size or floating airily in too generous space.

★ Work towards a consistent style, limiting yourself to certain typefaces and types of paper stock.

★ Estimate the time you can give to the project in actual hours available – you may find that a period of two weeks actually allows you only eight hours' free time – and work out how long things take you to do. Decide with the Chaser what overall timing is realistic.

★ Compile a list of people who can assist you – illustrators, photographers, typists etc.

More than the others, the skills involved in this role must be learnt. Everyone will be most impressed by even your most basic efforts. Deliberately tackle some small items first, but do not hesitate to accept the challenges as your skills will grow fast. Very soon you will be shaping the effect of a message, rather than barely coping with the deadline. It is out of that self-confidence that your church's unique style will emerge.

41

The Reporter

This title fairly reflects the job of carrying news of your planned appeals or events to all the networks that connect you to the audiences important to your church. If your team is short of bodies, the task can be added either to that of the Leader or the Forager. Should your ambitions as a group be large or your potential audiences many, try hard to fill this role. The right person can gain much free publicity and provide contacts which can themselves provide further support of all kinds, long into the future.

As described in the section called **Analyse Your Audience** on p 12, the Reporter should discover the available channels to all possible audiences – some in the professional media, others in local groups or with individuals – and then use them.

Does such a role suggest a rhino-skinned person? Someone full of energy and push? Not necessarily. Our cause is not commercial, our results described not only in targets attained but also in the quality of their doing. Let us make that difference clear. A professional public relations person will strive to convince clients to make assessments based on long-term results, but will usually be judged on short-term ones. Such an executive will have more than one such client at the same time, each demanding priority over the others. Thankfully, we can consider the needs of just one client (the church) and be patient about the results, knowing they will come all in God's good time.

Sometimes your Reporter will be asking the local newspaper to carry information on a forthcoming church event; sometimes he may try to get a journalist or photographer to cover it. Occasionally he will urge a local radio station to include one of your church speakers in a discussion programme, or to cooperate in some other way. Always, though, building relations with media will be no different from the normal human process of making friends. The Reporter will therefore always look towards deepening your church's relations with its audiences. This motive will

42

take him to other local churches to share your ideas and your news, as well as into the wider community.

The person you need must be at ease with people, able to ask for attention without demanding it and ready wherever possible to provide appropriate information. He must be thorough in filing names and addresses of all contacts, adding relevant facts that will remind him what matters to the other person. While the Reporter will often be the voice of your group, take care that you do not regard all contact as his sole property: where a different person can serve better as a spokesman in some particular case, arrange that – indeed, have your Reporter look for such opportunities.

Putting Your Team Together

It is for you to decide the ideal size for your team in the light of your needs and personality resources. More than eight individuals may easily become a bureaucracy, while fewer than eight will restrict any reasonably ambitious programme. Our survey of churches did suggest that most activities became dependent on a few activists, either due to numbers available to help or to poor recruiting. Perhaps some churches avoid the chore of drawing more men and women into such tasks, but we can accept that some parishes truly do not have the capacity and accordingly offer team-compositions of from four to eight members.

Group of 8	*Group of 7* (choice of role combinations)	
1. Leader	1. Leader/Reporter	1. Leader
2. Cashier	2. Cashier	2. Cashier
3. Forager	3. Forager	3. Forager/Reporter
4. Fixer	4. Fixer	4. Fixer
5. Chaser	5. Chaser	5. Chaser
6. Writer	6. Writer	6. Writer
7. Designer	7. Designer	7. Designer
8. Reporter		

Group of 6	Group of 5	Group of 4
1. Leader/Reporter	1. Leader/Reporter	1. Leader/Writer
2. Cashier	2. Cashier/Chaser	2. Cashier/Chaser
3. Forager/Chaser	3. Forager/Fixer	3. Forager/Reporter
4. Fixer	4. Writer	4. Designer/Fixer
5. Writer	5. Designer	
6. Designer		

Meetings of the whole group should be few and only for practical purposes. Even with eight members, given clear role definitions, meetings can concern two or three individuals at a time. The time for full meetings is after one event and before the next.

The combined roles suggested here are related to amounts of work normally generated. Please do not feel inhibited by the role titles here named. The labels used don't matter as long as they are clear and not over-dignified. If we can't communicate simply among ourselves, we have scant chance of doing so with our audiences.

Arrange Your Programme

One of the few occasions on which all your group should attend is the periodic planning session. According to what your church leadership has to say on policy, the Leader should outline a programme on paper – something brief and clear – and circulate it in advance to the specialists already recruited. For the first such meeting, prospective members can be included as observers – they'll be volunteers by the end of the meeting. Let this be an approximate programme, open enough for the meeting to change elements, to which end ask them to come with comments and ideas ready. Do not close the meeting until the programme is firm and all those going to participate are clearly enthused, and do not spin it out until everyone is exhausted.

It is helpful to agree the subjects and timing of the first two projects and to make them simple and quick. The success of these first messages will cement enthusiasm and commitment. Even at that time, pencil in the programme for one year ahead if you can. Set your team to clarifying every detail of costing, timing and production and have your plans for circulation of messages practical and well understood. Two or three of you, including the Leader and the Fixer, will need to meet several times to complete the full picture. Items must fall within the cash and budget allowed.

Between the first and second projects hold a full team meeting with a readiness to reallocate roles where people feel it would help. After that, as experience grows, the skills and the ambition open up.

The next part of this book uses a series of examples drawn from the actual experiences of different groups, condensed into the sorts of messages or events you may be doing yourselves.

Part II
Solving

Part II of this book will look at some typical church information and publicity activities, reconstructing the decision-making process. It attempts to show that in order to bring materials to life, you must seek to touch the recipients with God's Truth and with loving concern. It will conclude with a selection of ideas other groups of Christians have made work: some cover entire concepts; others show points of technique; several are amalgamations of similar answers found for the same questions. For many of the items to follow, credit must go to the churches who answered our request to send examples of their printed materials.

No rule declares how many messages make enough, nor what the composition of your year's programme ought to be. To some extent in all Christian traditions, the service itself is the message. Some churches do not choose to go much beyond this, while in others social action is a large part of the expression of the faith. Some are deliberately closer to the language and idiom of the day, others preferring to offer the message from a reserved position. In a few traditions, creative expression is restricted; meanwhile, some ecumenical groupings are developing new expression. Some churches follow a centralised line on communications; yet others work independently of their headquarters. This book permits us freedom to give advice without constant reference to denominational lines. Each message-maker therefore must adapt what seems useful to her group's own unique pattern of limitations and opportunities.

In a newsletter, Bryant Myers, drawing from his experience of working with Third World communities, writes,

The key to being successful servants of a community may lie in our capacity to identify what God is already doing in the community and to feel His pace and His sense of when times are full. We should endeavour to identify this ordained process of change and lay ours within it. How many times have we had the experience in our lives of being unable to pull something together or to understand something until a certain point in time where suddenly it all comes together, when the time was full?

With so many opportunities, the messages you make may well unleash an almost infinite number of demands for addresses, appropriate reference books to read – more data than this book has space for. For this reason, and the even better one that your group's maturing as good message-makers depends on your finding your own way, these pages offer stimulation, not automatic programmes, leaving your team to find its own way forward. Where possible, some addresses will be noted, but only a few. One indispensible reference book is a copy of the *UK Christian Handbook* (MARC Europe, every two years). Its Media section lists a number of Christian professional services, including Art & Layout, Audio Visual & Producers, Audio Cassette/Film/Filmstrip Libraries & Producers, Concert Organisers, Literature Producers & Distributors, Public Address Equipment Suppliers, Publishers, Radio & TV Programme Producers, Recording Services and Video Cassette Producers.

Beyond these sources, have your Reporter search the local Yellow Pages, consult the local chamber of commerce, check the local library and generally ask friends and colleagues. These are the kinds of information that your team needs to know if the sources are to become people.

The following examinations of basic Christian message-making activities act as starting points for your own thinking. By all means improve on them, then send us a copy please, so that it too may be shared with other Christian groups.

The Parish Periodical

If you discern a certain guardedness in the wording of this heading, you are right. The item we now consider may be issued monthly, weekly or fortnightly – even intermittently. It may run from two sides only to any number of pages. It may be typewritten or professionally typeset. It may carry preprinted covers, sections or inserts. It may be as small as 5⅞″ × 8¼″ or as big as a newspaper. It may serve one church, a circuit of churches or an ecumenical association of churches. It may be all information, all homily, or a mixture. Its tone may be intense or almost flippant. It may come free or priced from 5p to 50p. It may be the work of one person or of many. And it may be called a magazine, a bulletin, a sheet, an update, a newsletter, a message ... or nothing at all. Yet its purpose, at least, is common: every parish needs a regular organ of communication with its actual and potential church-goers; every parish needs a regular, recognisable piece which is the outward, topical expression of its religious and social life, one which keeps the Christian presence alive and available and – as an important secondary benefit – acts as a pressure to get other church decisions made on time. It must carry a timetable of events, name people for special duties and state the venues for group meetings; knowing the parish periodical (PP) is due out, committees tend to clarify many details.

Your church will have such a PP. The first question is whether its format, timing and method of production become a straight-jacket. Here are four more. Is its production limited to one person's efforts, and if so, for reasons of time-pressure only? When you compare the latest edition with the oldest you can find, is the experience one of *dèja-vu?* Has nothing changed in your church's life, and is everything as predictable as the seasons of the church year? Are you allowing expediency and sheer habit to enshrine the editorial style and layout, making the assumption that it is the parishioner's job to work for understanding, not yours to awaken it?

The balance of the familiar and the unexpected is for you to decide, but try not to use the excuse of time-pressure as a refuge. You can do as some churches do and alternate the teams who put the PP together. It is open to you to vary the format, even the size, depending on cost. You may consider keeping the standard issue down to fewer pages and less ambition, while periodically publishing a more dramatic 'special'. 'Specials' can be designed to reach a wider audience than the standard issues, perhaps tackling particular subjects in greater depth and so linking up with your programme of events. Using 'specials' as vehicles for advertising events is well worth considering.

Once those fundamental decisions have been made, think again about your PP's title. Does it express the purpose of your message-making? Does it actually name your church clearly and give its full postal address? One in three of our researched sample somewhat cavalierly assumed that all readers would already know such things.

Your group should at this stage review the purposes of the PP. To what extent is it merely keeping your regulars warm? To what extent does it speak to potential new members? (Surely, every 'special' at least ought to open a door to those who are looking for Jesus?). Think about which audiences you reach and decide to make the PP relevant to them; should messages for members *and* the wider community go in the same issue, or special issues be planned for each

49

distinct audience? Discuss together the impact of the PP on particular audiences, trying to think it through from their perspectives. Does it seem formal or friendly? Does its language truly reflect your church, or not? Is it talking to or at the reader? Is the tone amicable or patronising? Do you want to change any of those things?

Next, review the physical limitations. Are you locked into a print process because you own a machine or have made a contract? If so, can you choose the page size or type of paper used? If you are free to reconsider format and printing method, ask your Fixer to investigate costs and options. It is likely that such things have not been changed in your church for some years, while technology has been changing almost daily. Once your Fixer reports back, the Forager can set about getting the printing or the paper donated by some local businesses. For this purpose, a typed analysis of costs should be offered, broken down as per issue and annually; give also separate figures for the paper cost, the preprinted covers' cost, the reproduction cost, the editorial expenses (postage etc). If the Forager cannot find sponsors for the whole cost, he can set about getting pledges to cover parts of it. It is possible to have a pattern of sponsorship throughout the year – and nothing prompts a businessman to cooperation more quickly than seeing a competitor's name already given as a sponsor. Sometimes this sponsorship approach can produce more income than the direct offer of advertisement space, the ad 'coming gratis' as a thank-you – not as a condition – for the sponsorship.

A significant element in any PP may be the presence of a stapled-in preprinted centre section, such as are routinely prepared by some churches' denominational headquarters, by the diocese, perhaps, or from some other editorial source. Your Leader, Writer and Designer should rethink quite how this cuckoo is affecting their nest. If it is carrying the main responsibility for presenting the Christian message, should the parish produced outer pages duplicate that intention, or seek to contrast it? If its tone is formal or authoritative,

50

should they echo it? As the inset will be a professionally typeset and designed piece – giving a denser appearance with more words to the page than can be achieved legibly with typewriting – should they look to build in some continuity, for instance by matching headline typefaces or column arrangement, or by blending the parish pages' written style with it? Or should they accept the differences as 'light and shade' and set about increasing them?

You may wish first to conduct a 'reading and noting' survey among regular PP readers. The Reporter or the Chaser might do this to assess which items are important and which are less so. It can help you improve the allocation of space, order the items more helpfully, identify those which are redundant, even indicate those which are missing. Approach a number of regular PP readers: at least 10% would be ideal. Balance your sample so that it includes a representative spread. Visit each person, saying that you are improving the PP and need help. In the first questions the person is asked to list the items that interest him. Write these down in the order given, without comment. It is important that the person does not feel under test, or that there are right and wrong answers. Tell him that his answers will not remain under his name, but 'go in the pot'. Once the answers peter out, read through a prepared list of items, pausing for reactions. You can mark the list on a 1,2,3 rating scale (no interest, some interest, high interest). Having reached the stage of prompted responses, run back through the headings, asking if the person can recall particular items from the past issues; if the recalled item involved a mention of a family member, circle the mark you put on the rating scale. Ask him to give his preferred three items in order. Last of all invite him to suggest items that *should* be included. Limit these additional questions as the answers will become less useful the longer the interview goes on. Asking about the cover price (if any) may be useful, whereas asking about the design will be unproductive. Asking about how often the issues should be published will usually elicit the answer that everyone thinks it comes out more often

51

than it really does – a defence-mechanism arising from the fact that people may feel guilty about not reading it from cover to cover.

Such a survey can only be a rough guide to what the PP contents should be, to where they should be positioned and what length they should be. If those interviewed mention items that were *not* in the latest issue you asked them to read, pay attention; for unless you suspect they did not read the issue, it suggests that such an item is of importance to them. It will almost certainly open your eyes to what you have been doing and confirm for the poor Writer that not everybody reads everything he offers. Look up items often praised to see what it was you were doing right.

The Leader should assemble all the responses and from them prepare a fresh brief for the PP to discuss with the team. The Writer must be clear about the intended readers, sure that the style of writing is appropriate to them *and* to the character of the church. The Designer can work with the Fixer to establish the practical print-process, after which she should prepare a layout of a grid to show how the columns of text will fit and what kind of heading typefaces might be used. The pictorial content should be agreed. Will you concentrate on photos, locally produced drawings, 'swipes' from Christian News Service, or a combination? Fully discuss this last element as it profoundly alters the impact of your PP. Also, see guidelines given for assembling the text, p 150.

The Chaser must have a list of contributors and take over the tough task of getting items in before the print deadline. Let the Writer ask people to write things, then let the Chaser collect them – that way the Writer stays on easy terms with his contributors. The Reporter must check with the Writer well in advance as to which items might merit a wider exposure in the local media; conversely, the Reporter should also be making contributions on the basis of what impact the church's message-making is having in the community.

Except at the planning stage, the Leader should limit full team meetings about the PP to special editions. Apart from

52

this, as few people as possible should be discussing progress.

The Forager can look for talents as well as free materials – a local photographer, a free shed to house the group's printing machine.

The Cashier should work with the Fixer to control costs, but also to establish correct spending levels for departures from the norm such as 'specials' or new PP formats.

A Sample Schedule for a Parish Periodical

(P-Day Publication Day)

P-Day minus 12 months Select outer covers for full year if using preprinted covers, or redesign.

P-Day minus 6 months Sell advertising space for next six issues at special rate.

P-Day minus 3 months Editor to decide next three months' themes.

P-Day minus 28 days Sell small ads for coming edition. Call for written contributions; suggest subjects; provide word-count; brief for extra contributions to cover possible gaps.

P-Day minus 14 days Chase contributors of text; brief illustrators – artists or photographers – locate 'swipes' – ready-printed items you are free to use on your artwork.

P-Day minus 7 days Edit text; type it up in galley form; get someone else to check it; chase up advertisers' copy or artwork; review current church activities in case something vital has been missed.

P-Day minus 4 days Assemble artwork or prepare stencils.

P-Day minus 2 days Get someone else to double-check artwork; alter as necessary; add-in stop-press news only if vital.

P-Day Deliver to printer or repro person. Pray as usual!

Some Promptings

Consider a larger page size and therefore fewer pages; it might make your PP look more interesting and allow the Designer freedom to use larger pictures. On an A4 format you can set it up in two or three columns, while on A5 only 1 or 2 are possible. (See list of paper sizes on p 155.) As a general rule narrower columns are read more readily than very wide ones. Learn from the newspapers and put in a subhead every 30 lines or so (around 200) words. Compare notes with other churches; you may be able to pool talents and resources – typewriters, printing machines etc. Consider sharing the bulk buying of paper. Consider a directory of small advertisements – space for space, small ads bring in more revenue than display ads. Think of your PP as an ambassador for your church: it should make a good substitute for a personal contact, but if it comes nowhere near, rethink the whole thing.

Several organisations provide catalogues of pre-printed pages or sections which allow local PPs to have full-colour covers at low cost or editorial content they could not themselves manage. Some addresses:

Church News Service 37B New Cavendish Street, London W1M 8JR. A rich source of news, features, quotes, jokes and illustrations – but beware: don't become too dependent or it won't remain *your* PP. It comes out monthly and serves 5000 churches of all denominations.

Concordia 28 Huntingdon Road, Cambridge CB3 0HH. Tel: (0223) 65113. A full, colourful range of covers, samples of which are available on request. You can order as few as 50 or in thousands. Note that they supply the covers flat and that they are *not* quite A4, but 8½" × 11".

Challenge Literature Fellowship Revenue Buildings, Chapel Road, Worthing, West Sussex BN11 1BQ. Tel: (0903) 200775. They supply four-colour A4 leaflets supplied flat and ready for overprinting for such subjects as 'Easter Story', also a tabloid newspaper which you can order from a number of options to use as 'specials'. You may take this 4-page paper as it is with some of your local news in a special panel; take the panel plus the front page; use the centre spread for your own material; or take pages 2, 3 and 4, using their front page. They can typeset from your copy. Minimum orders vary from 2000-5000.

Christian Literature Press Unit 206–207, Springvale Industrial Estate, Cwmbran, Gwent. Tel: (063 33) 60998. They don't do covers or formal inserts but do provide a range of invitation cards suitable for every church activity, your PP perhaps making a good vehicle when such a church event is planned.

The Office (London) Ltd 5 Crown Close, London E3 2JQ. They produce 'Clip-Art' books for Sunday School and Youth Worker purposes. These may be useful as a source of 'swipes'.

Christian Publicity Organisation Garcia Estate, Canterbury Road, Worthing BN13 1BW. Tel: (0903) 64556. They do not produce materials for PPs but have such a wide range of other items, from leaflets to posters, for everyone from pastors to children, that you might like to ask for their list.

Bible Lands Society PO Box 50, High Wycombe, Bucks HP15 7QU. Tel: (0494) 21351. Widely used by churches for PP covers and other ready-for-overprinting purposes.

Redemptorist Publications Alphonsus House, Chawton, Alton, Hants GU34 3BR. Tel: (0420) 88222. A service for Roman Catholic churches providing a great range of publications, the most used of which are the weekly parish sheets, printed on one side with a two-colour design and Christian teaching on a seasonal theme, leaving the other side for service details and local subject matter.

Victory Tracts & Posters Portland Road, London SE25 4PN. Tel: 01-656 2297. Though they do not provide materials specifically for PPs, they will give permission for tract material to be used as long as source is acknowledged.

Other sources: Christian Printers' Fellowship, High Street, Rowhedge, Colchester, Essex C05 7HG. Tel: (0206) 867367. Home Words Ltd., PO Box 44, Guildford GU1 1XI. A R Mowbray & Co Ltd, St Thomas House, Becket Street, Oxford OX1 1SJ.

These sources may well provide your PP with some 'instant' sophistication, save you some time, help decorate your pages. Again, do not allow their convenience to limit your group's development in finding an expression unique to your own church.

The Christian Event Promotion

The subject of fundraising comes up later in this part of the book (see p 76-83). Here we are concerned with activities designed to dramatise the spiritual life of the church. You will need to decide at the outset what result is desired: to consolidate the commitment of your regular church-goers or attract a wider group. Is the event aimed at one age range? From a limitless choice of events we here concentrate on just one, leaving you to adapt its lessons to any other you may prefer. Whichever event is chosen, let it relate to a clear understanding of the audience concerned. As has been said earlier, to go for general audiences is to waste money and to speak to no-one in particular.

In this example, a church's membership – or the typical regular churchgoer – is too heavily concentrated in the middle-aged to elderly range. It is vital to attract younger Christians, so these become the declared target for the church's messages. That's fine; now you know what the church wants, but do you know what *they* want? Are there younger people in your group of message-makers? If so, how young? Obviously, you can act only with what you have. If you want to attract teenagers, but have nobody of that age range who can give you the necessary insights, how can you meet them, speak with them, and attract them onto your ground? Seeing that you are not prepared for that age-group, you decide that your best chance is to aim for people aged 25 to 35. With a few in your membership in that age range, you make them your contact team. They do not necessarily have to run the activity but serve as the bridge to the target group. Ask them to brief the rest of you, giving a picture of what it's like to be that age. Understand what responsibilities they bear, what ages their children are likely to be, what spare time they have, where their tensions, their hopes, their frustrations are. Find out what leisure time these couples can find together, and what apart. Try to identify where this age range tends to congregate in your area. Are they in the new estates, the bed-sits, the furnished flats, the maisonettes? From this process alone, many ideas can arise; your group should note every thought for later discussion. Let's say that your group discovers that, yours being an urban parish, you have many young couples and that they fall into two main groups: those who started families young and those who have delayed children in favour of careers. In all communications, the more identifiable the group, the greater is the chance of making a strong contact; but this equation also means smaller numbers. For businessmen, this can often be a disadvantage because they need to work on a large scale; for you, it is an advantage. After discussion, you select the second group — those who have begun their families later to establish careers. You perceive a number of needs arising from the pressures of this way of life, and most of them are the wives'. They may feel under-challenged intellectually, even if content with their physical lives. They may be afraid their husbands will lose respect for them, that they must now 'fall behind' in the career race. You decide that these people must need spiritual nurture and set about drawing them into church life, ultimately as couples bringing their children into the church family. The medium for all this is the wives' needs.

A sweep of options is open to you. Setting up a special club is considered, but rejected as being too formal a solution. A lunch-time lecture series is rejected, as it was feared that attracting a consistently high standard of speaker might prove impossible. Coffee mornings and the like are thought to be too 'cosy' for these women, who will be sensitive to any hint of a patronising approach. Such participatory interests as music, dance, art or drama are liked, but regarded as too specialised to please a fairly large group. You do conclude, however, that some element of challenge is useful, yet within a framework that will not deter the less self-confident. Someone says, 'Relationships matter here,' and someone else says, 'They're trying to understand their roles in life.' At last you hit on a formula: a video show with talk. Many inner city and town authorities are introducing videotape lending into their libraries at a day-rate substantially lower than charged by retailers. Using the library's list, you select a set of feature films, ideally offering subjects centred on contemporary family relationships in settings familiar to these women. These videos should provoke discussion on religious principles; they may be forthright in nature as they deal with topics of fidelity, the 'battle of the sexes' or any other relevant subject. You do not look for films that provide a comfortable moral ending, because it is in the very nature of the tensions so rehearsed that the ground of a spiritual need may be discovered.

There are now practicalities to be considered. When, where and how often should the events happen? How many women make up an audience? If some men locally are accepting a role reversal and staying at home to look after the children, should they be encouraged to attend? Your contact people very sensibly suggest a trial run. (The Writer muses aloud that a 'Dummy Run' might make a great sponsored event, but this is not popular.) The Fixer wants to talk numbers. You agree that ten to twelve would be about right and that, since you are approaching people not known to you, the commercial 'cold-canvass' response expectation of 3% would suggest you err on the side of caution and expect a ratio of 50 invitations per 1 acceptance. A batch of 500 invitations is duly prepared. By way of a test, 100 of them are personally addressed by name after consulting the electoral roll, while the remainder are marked 'Do you care about your relationships?'; all will be hand delivered. In each envelope will also be included a spare invitation 'for your partner or a friend', as it is agreed that some of the women might be more prepared to come if they don't have to be alone. The wording of the invitation is approved by the Leader: To create a sense of participation, the message asks the recipient to choose which of three feature films she would prefer; there is a tear-off coupon with room for the title tick-boxes, name and address and telephone number. On the personalised 100, the team will hand-write the person's name and address in the coupon to see if that will spur extra response. The wording offers a free video show in the church annexe, indicating that no more than twenty people would attend, that coffee and informal conversation is to follow. The date and time are given. By offering a 'vote' on which film should be shown, response is encouraged. By not asking for a firm commitment to attend at this stage, some otherwise reticent women will be drawn in.

The Cashier is concerned about recovering costs, and it is agreed that, at the end of the first video show when those attending will be invited to a second show, donations towards the costs will be sought. The invitation card challenges the women to come to terms with the big dangers to modern marriages, making it clear that a dialogue of discovery is in store, not a preaching. The Designer finds a leaflet for one of the films (*Kramer versus Kramer*) and adds a message discussing the importance of the video show at the church. The Reporter takes a copy of this to the local paper, and the editor promises to publish it in the appropriate edition – timed to appear when the leaflets are delivered. The Forager arranges the borrowing of the video player and for permission to show the video, getting a retailer to loan a large projection screen on the basis that his shop's cards would be handed round, and finds someone else to donate the refreshments.

The Fixer has planned the door-to-door delivery in selected local streets, briefing the leafleteers to do their round once the morning sun is well up and to look for homes showing signs of having children – prams or push-chairs on the path, for example. They are briefed on the scheme so that if questioned they can be encouraging. The contact team –

those whose ages match those of the target audience – are put on standby to answer telephone calls, their home numbers being used in the invitation card.

After 10 days the responses are analysed. If the return is big, more than one meeting can be arranged; which videos are shown will depend on the response received. Now the contact people must follow-up the returned coupons or calls in person, formally inviting them to the event by handing over tickets with the name hand-written in. When calling it is important for the contact person to note the names of children – and any other facts that can help make the eventual show a success for the women attending.

Meanwhile, the Leader is already considering, in consultation with the Chaser, what follow-up activity might be successful having secured the women's interest, to widen out from discussion only to other events based perhaps on non-fiction videos presented by experts from the field of family relationships. The end is to secure a family's involvement with the church. It is for the Leader and the clergyman (who may well be one and the same) to decide on when and how these events will be given the spiritual dimension. At one level, a 'filter' has already been applied, as the recipients of the invitations will certainly have recognised its Christian identity. Some will be tentative, being unfamiliar or apprehensive about a church setting. You decide you must let them come to you as a result of seeing the relevance of faith during the reassessment of their own lives in discussion. These women will need to feel that any decisions are *theirs*. You do not plan it fully, waiting to see what is most needed, but intend to look for some way to give individuals a private opportunity for counsel.

Seeing how the thought process has worked through this example, examine now which kind of target group is important to your church, remaining open to individuals' needs as *they* see them. People simply cannot conduct two conversations at once. Their conversation with God can begin in earnest when the confused one about their practical problems has been partially stilled, scaled down to a controllable level.

Such an activity will confirm how much better it is to confine our efforts to groups with whom we can establish intimately personal terms. We must then trust that the Lord will speak to their hearts.

'Join the Family' Activity

Moving into a new district is an exciting, yet disorienting experience. For practising Christians, the locating of a suitable church will be a priority; for nominal or lapsed Christians, the new life represented by a change of home may also open the way to a new spiritual life. Short of constantly prowling the streets in pursuit of removal vans, what can a church group do to meet this need? There is certainly a good case for co-operative action here among local churches, jointly welcoming newcomers in a demonstration of Christian harmony. For families already committed to a particular denomination this will prove no impediment; for those as yet uncommitted, an open invitation to attend a number of different churches will seem most welcoming.

To this end, a 'welcome pack' including separate invitations from a number of local pastors, ministers, vicars and priests may stimulate a return to the fold at the right psychological moment.

Where such joint action is impractical, what might your church do individually? As always, think first about the situation of your target family. How will they feel? At what point will they be ready to consider involvement *outside* their new home? Which offers will be helpful and which will seem an unnecessary burden? Remember that people in a new environment may wish to pause, take a deep breath and consider hard before re-immersing themselves in a social network. Timing is therefore important. Somebody appearing on the doorstep while the furniture is coming in may be considered a busybody. Someone calling during the dazed, empty feelings of a day later just to pass over a welcome pack and shake a hand is likely to be appreciated. Before you plan the message, though, you should develop an intelligence network. You need to know when people are moving in, yet short of creating a 'commisar' system where you have a person on every street reporting comings and goings, how can you tell when and where to offer your welcome? Local estate agents or solicitors engaged in house conveyancing could help. They may not be prepared to divulge even general information if they feel it impinges on their clients confidentiality, and if it is stored in machine readable format, they legally cannot, anyway, so ask them instead kindly to pass on or mail on a welcome pack to the incoming family. (See information about data protection, p 15). If the pack is prepared in such a way that it can only please the recipient, the action can only reflect credit on their firms. If necessary, consider a barter whereby you include their addresses in the church magazine's directory of local professional firms. Failing that, you can obtain regular lists of properties for rent or sale from estate agents simply by asking to receive them. And of course, your church people can always keep an eye on the sale boards, waiting for the 'sale agreed' and 'sold' signs before asking one of the nearby neighbours to pass the pack over on your behalf a couple of days after someone's moved in. If at all possible, aim to put the family's name on the address label, although something like 'Welcome, new neighbours' will obviously do.

What should go into a welcome pack? The possibilities range from a plain letter of welcome all the way to a gift carton of the kind that first-time mothers are sometimes given by baby product manufacturers. This last idea is worth adapting by persuading local retailers each to give an item towards a Just Moved in Survival Kit – again in return for entries in the local services directory of your magazine. Alternatively, ask them each to contribute a voucher towards a stapled book of them, all offering a percentage off a first item purchase. Your group can duplicate these onto different coloured papers to make the voucher-book look attractive. You don't need to barter for this; after all, you're bringing in new potential customers for them. If your Forager is keen, everyone from the local newsagent to the local baby-sitter can make an introductory offer.

As part of the same pack could be one or both of two printed items: the *Welcome Card* and the church *Who's Who*.

The Welcome Card Print this on a card of sufficient quality that the new family won't want to throw it away, and the card will not deteriorate if kept handy for reference. Big printers often have offcuts from long runs of expensive jobs; if you ask the manager, he'll probably let your Forager pick them up from time to time. You won't need too many, at most 100 a year. It should carry a message of welcome from the clergyman, introducing the church community, for which your Writer gives him a word-count. The Designer can make 250 words or less look bold and easy to read, much more becomes an essay. The Reporter gets an Ordnance Survey map of the parish and a version of this is prepared, adding the key services a newcomer to the district would need to know, including the location of the church. Put in everything useful from the GP to the dentist, from the nearest swimming pool to the numbers of the buses and where the stops are, from the bakers to the shoe menders, from the location of the schools to the places the telephone booths and the post-boxes are. Have the location of the incoming family's home marked with an arrow. Your Designer puts a cheerful design on the cover making the welcome; on the inside left page is the pastor's letter; on the opposite page is the map and on the back a list of your church's contact addresses, details of your church clubs and groups, and the times of services. Inserted in the card on a slip of coloured paper is a typed invitation for the family to the coming weekend's morning service, where a blessing for their new home can be given.

The Church Who's Who Most churches produce a telephone directory of their members, giving it a limited circulation and spending very little time or money on it. It serves a limited purpose. A *Who's Who* is more than that. Its purpose is to put faces to the people, and it offers two distinct advantages: it helps cement the loyalty of existing members by demonstrating their involvement, and it helps make your church community more accessible to newcomers. It can be part of the welcome pack if you judge that to be right, or it might be used as a follow-up piece carrying a note reminding them they'd be welcome to the next family service. This second approach could encourage some shy people to come along, and make others – who might discount the first contact – take your church more seriously. What they will most certainly do is check up what the face that goes with the signature on the note actually looks like – so make sure there's a smile. The *Who's Who* can be free to new neighbours as long as the cost is covered by charging the regular members the basic cost price every time you give an updated issue.

How to go about making one? The Leader decides how much information about a person makes enough. Is it necessary to print ages? Should a person's occupation be described (a) generally – 'shopkeeper', (b) particularly – 'owner of knitting shop', or (c) not at all? Should families be grouped? Should the office-holders of the church be grouped apart? What kind of personal biographical detail should be included? The formula is important. A *Who's Who* that talks about people in terms of their qualities and their service serves a very different purpose to the one which segregates people in secular terms.

If there is no photographer available to you from among your congregation, your Forager starts looking for a local photo business which might be encouraged to offer free or at-cost services, a good starting point being those who regularly get commissions to cover weddings at the church. All you need ask of them is to come periodically after a morning service and shoot a roll of 35mm black and white film (36 frames), or make some Polaroid instant prints. As a last

64

resort, find someone with a basic Polaroid you can borrow. Every so often, when you judge that about a dozen to sixteen new people are joining worship at the church, ask the Reporter to gather them after a service and have the photographer set up his tripod at some well-lit, quiet spot in the church grounds or in a porch, and take two shots each of the people.

Here's how you could handle it: The Fixer has a set of forms prepared, each with the person's name written in. After the photograph, the person and the form are passed over to the Reporter who then enters the remainder of the information, the person signing the sheet to approve the details. This whole process takes under an hour. The sheets are marked with the same numbers as the sequence of film frames used so that forms and faces will match up. The Chaser takes care of this minor piece of administration, collecting from the photographer the one strip of contact prints he makes from the negatives. The Designer cuts out each photo-frame – all of which are head and shoulder shots showing relaxed faces – picking the best of the two pictures in every case for the *Who's Who*; the spare is filed with the Chaser as a reserve, marked with the person's name. The Designer now prepares a basic layout grid by ruling-up a horizontal A4 sheet (see A). The information is then typed direct onto the sheet in the appropriate panel, the Writer editing the Reporter's fact sheet down to a standard number of words. Onto this grid (see B) the Designer now glues the photo-frames, the Chaser doing the final checking for accuracy. Care is taken to leave clear margins all round and down the centre gulley of the sheet before each sheet is photocopied on a machine which will not degrade the tone of the prints. Once a full set of sheets is assembled, each is slit down the centre to make an A5 sheet. Although it is more economical to print on both sides of the sheet, this will throw the *Who's Who* out of chronological order. Your Designer decides that a loose-leaf system is more flexible than anything stapled, allowing replacements or additional sheets to be supplied later and easily fitted in. Each sheet is numbered for this reason. To contain each *Who's Who* a C5 white envelope has its top flap cut off to make a sleeve; a sticker is typed to go on the front, with the title and room for the recipient's name to be entered. When each latest batch is assembled they are distributed by the Fixer and the fact recorded by the Chaser.

To update entries, the Designer has a reasonably simple job. When church members leave the district or die, she may act in different ways. Those who have simply moved house can eventually be deleted when the periodic update is due. At that time, with the aid of a scalpel and some Cow Gum glue, the Designer can close up items. At such times, the Writer can take the opportunity, in consultation with the Reporter, to review the biographical wording, check the address details and so on. Indeed, the Reporter or Chaser should be noting such alterations during the year. In the case of a person's death, you might like to follow the example of some churches who leave the picture in with an *in memoriam* paragraph, at least until the following update. An alternative to this approach is to remove the deceased from the current *Who's Who* and transfer them to a leatherbound memorial book, with the addition of a favourite text, a hymn verse, or a prayer. Different traditions will treat this subject in very different ways, so no advice will be given here as to style, except to warn against the inclination to give the *Who's Who* the chatty presentation of a family snapshot album; whimsical or over-jovial wording will date the piece dreadfully. Set a consciously steady style, as engaging as seems appropriate, then stick to it.

Christian Stewardship Development

A Christian's commitment to faith is hardly something that can be stuck with a pin, labelled and date-stamped. The condition of active faith is affected by private and congregational religious experience and by the general joys and jarrings of everyday life. The picture of what a person's

Christian commitment should be will vary from church to church, some traditions having formal membership rules or a rigid code, others encouraging a good deal of individual inter-pretation. The use of the suggestions that follow will be adapted to suit your church's conception of such matters.

Most churches rely on their regular worshippers for the very substance of their survival and growth, out of which arises an important challenge. On the one hand, would you settle for a 'membership subs' arrangement, where cash-giving is graded by age or relative affluence and becomes regarded as a special bill among other domestic bills to be paid each week or month? This tithing approach has its appeal. It reduces personal embar-rassment to a minimum at both ends of the transaction, and it makes your church treasurer very happy to have a reliable cashflow. More than that, by locking a family's giving to the concept of membership, then loyalty and commitment merge into habit, the breaking with which becomes harder as time passes. The spiritual aspect of such tithing we will not rehearse here.

On the other hand—and this is the position less beloved of church treasurers—would you prefer such commitment to be a live, conscious, if riskier, issue? Would you see a person's giving of time, talents or resources an expression of faith made stronger by the need constantly to reaffirm the decision? Quite where on this spectrum your church positions its stewardship campaign will depend on a mix of its traditional view and on local realities. Yet there are some common denominators which may be shared here.

First, put aside any idea that collecting the commitment is in any way an undue pressure on the Christian individual. The process is one of presenting an opportunity. Your team's part in this is an enabling one. Ultimately, the temporal responsibility and the satisfaction is all the giver's. It is his faith that stands in need of tangible expression and if this is a contract at all, it is one with the Lord. As I Chronicles 29:14 tells us: 'But who am I, and who are my people, that we should be able to give as generously as this? Everything comes from you, and we have given you only what comes from your hand.' King David spoke these words in a state of joy, not mean defensiveness, and we can take our tone from his. We can view the individual who is in receipt of these gifts and resources (and the church through which he may offer them back to God) as stops along a railway line. There is a discipline involved, a timetable, a train to catch, a place to go. A stewardship scheme forms a part of the track. The ticket to ride is faith.

Second, following from David's words, do whatever is necessary to create a mood of pleasure in the building and running of your scheme. If ever it becomes a dread to its guardians, that mood will immediately transmit itself to the givers.

Third, spread as widely as possible the running of the scheme. This is certainly not to say that everyone should know how much others give. (In our society and probably in all the others before it, such matters are granted a hallowed privacy). (See again p 15 on data protection.) But the more people you can involve, each working with a small group, the less a 'them and us' mentality is likely to develop.

Time, Talents and Resources

It is often supposed that in these words the whole case has been made for stewardship. Your team must, however, relate them sensitively to the particular individuals you hope to involve. Each prospective participant will harbour at least two views of stewardship's components. *Time*, which is usually understood as spare or free time, is measurable in hours, may be shaped or shoehorned into rotas and duty lists; but it also has an emotional context. For a pensioner, time may be unfillable, while for a busy worrier it may be a crowded Babel. Avoid the assumption, 'You must have at least four hours a week free, so here is a responsibility exactly four hours long to fit you.' Much better to say, 'Here is a fulfilling task. You decide its worth and give it the time it needs.' Do not allow a dialogue to develop where excuses are offered or demanded, nor let anyone behave judgementally or use the leverage of comparing the commitment of others with that of the person you are asking.

The same applies to *talents*. Not everyone can be an opera singer or a financial wizard, and even if you were dealing with such talented parishioners, that is not to say that the service you would ask them to perform need be so grand. More humble tasks might suit them better, such people often finding satisfaction from the exercise of secondary, low-profile skills. Almost everyone has some simple social talent to offer: some will have practical abilities and energy to offer, others can turn their hobby interests to good effect. In expressing the church's needs, work to illuminate the opportunities in such a way that the talents are offered, not press-ganged.

Resources in this materialistic century tend to mean money. Let us quickly put money in its place. It makes things possible, certainly, and is handier than a votive offering of goats, but is no more important than time, talents or prayers. And when given reluctantly it burdens all. Think very carefully before giving comparative values to time, talents and money as you approach givers. Aim for a gift of all three. Someone putting in a weekend's work varnishing pews should see no trade-off between the hours so given and the total he puts in the weekly gift envelope. That would just undervalue the working time and make a barter of what should be from the heart. Likewise, two hours' deep prayer is not negotiable. If the giving is offered with joy, there is no calculation or comparison.

Purposes

Your message-makers must think carefully about how to give expression to the purpose of your stewardship scheme. Its overall aims – to promote mission and service to the glory of God, – while undeniable, are concepts difficult for people to keep constantly in mind. Conversely, purposes expressed in terms of 'housekeeping' – new hymn books or the church roof restoration – allow participants to see a practical and achievable objective but may allow them to lose sight of a higher motivation. The ideal formula is one in which a series of medium and longer-term objectives are given milestones – short- term stages towards the grander purpose. They offer the vital reinforcement that comes from success and can be seen in relation to bigger aims such as increasing church attendance, or bringing Bible study to wider groups.

When possible, such aims should be explained in terms of what might be achieved as well as what the costs will be. Suppose your aim is to attract younger people. Be brave; state a target for this year and how many for the year after; then indicate what religious and social changes or provisions this growth will impose. Involve your givers in that dream; make it their goal, too – a shared picture of where your church family is going. If they accept the challenge, the giving becomes not secondary but incidental.

Actions

There are three main ways to establish a stewardship scheme. Each has its value, and indeed, within your own church denomination, there may be an established formula based upon one of them. These ways may be understood as (a) the centralised way, (b) the steward's way, and (c) the shared way. The centralised way is centred on the clergy issuing a challenge and circulating leaflets/questionnaires designed to recruit the various forms of commitment. At its most centralised it can all be done via envelopes, lists on notice boards and spoken reminders during services; at its less formal, the clergy, with helpers, can make a programme of home visitations to secure commitment. The steward's way uses a team of challengers who will systematically approach church people, either through individual home visits by appointment or by 'at-homes' where perhaps four or five couples will be invited for refreshments and a presentation. The shared way literally involves the entire church membership, each family group or single member being asked to present the opportunity for commitment to one other family or single member.

In planning for any one of these methods, a system to record committment needs devising. This record will not be open to general view, though anyone must be able to see her own file upon demand. The church treasurer (or the Cashier if the message-making group is deputed to run the scheme) must keep a record of income paid and due, and one person – perhaps your Chaser – will need to keep the commitment record of time, talent and prayers. At regular intervals, probably annually, everybody who so commits should be given a copy of her commitments and invited to confirm it, increase it – even reduce it – in the clear understanding that the giving is between her and God. (Again see note on Data Protection p 15).

These three ways are not mutually exclusive, and you may have local reasons for combining elements. This book will discuss the last of the three ways, assuming, as always, that your group will adapt its elements to suit the realities of your local situation.

The Shared Stewardship Your team meets to plan the framework and the printed materials. It is agreed that a period of six weeks is needed to carry the campaign from announce-ment stage to commitment stage. The first two weeks will be used to generate interest and enthusiasm at the church, to complete lists of names and to include new members. Little needs to be explained at this stage about the form stewardship commitment may take. This is the time to express aims, to set priorities and to give a spiritual basis for the campaign. In the days before a launch at a main service dedicated to the scheme, the team sifts the names into geographical districts; as yours is a sprawling parish, you make more divisions to avoid long treks for anyone. Now each batch of names-by-location are considered. Within a family group, the identities of adults, younger people and

71

children are established. For this campaign you have decided that stewardship is for the 17-21s as one group and for the over-21s as another (though some churches prefer a 12-18 or 12-18+ split). Thus two separate lists are made. Name-matching then takes place when, from within one group and within one district, each person is allocated at least one other whom he is to contact. The matching then is by age, proximity and – where possible – by type of person.

This planning takes time, and the Leader makes decisions where disagreement arises. The Fixer now prepares individual packs. Each recipient is to get a leaflet explaining the purposes of stewardship, an action or pledge card (see below p 73-76), and a return envelope for later use. In addition, there will be a letter from the clergyman proposing that the recipient should contact a person named; the address and telephone number are supplied. The letter explains that the visit to this person is to help in the commitment of stewardship, and that the visitor's task will be just to offer counsel and to collect a sealed envelope containing a signed action card, later to deliver it to the church in time for a specified family service. Two other vital pieces of information must be included. One is that the visitor will be expected as the person to be visited will have been notified. The other is that soon the visitor will himself be receiving a visitor to elicit his *own* commitment; this other visitor's name is also given.

Your group chooses to arrange everything in a single letter, though two stages are possible. The response to this pattern of events is interesting. Some people are more than willing to help, but, rather than go through a formula they have already thought through, are anxious to complete their own action cards and get them direct to the church. As each person has to consider helping another, this naturally acts as a spur to his own actions. Discourage this haste if you can, however, as the quality of commitment is much deeper when shared with another person.

The Fixer notes which action cards (sometimes called

pledge cards) are not yet in and alerts the Chaser to follow-up the visitors concerned. With reminders given in church, along with group reports on progress, a full set should be collected within the month. As everyone has been involved, morale is high at this point and almost anything is possible for your church. Particularly sensitive pastoral care should be taken with non-respondents. No whiff of disapproval must occur. A useful approach here is to ask such people individually if they will perform some single chore as a favour – lock up the church grounds on the one night the usual office-holder can't manage it; or call on an old lady nearby with a message. Something small and uncommitted to any repetition. It will remove a sense of damaging guilt for non-participation in the main scheme and may well result in the person volunteering later to join in. If not, be patient and draw him or her gently towards the idea of Christian service in whatever ways are possible. This is a loving process.

Your Stewardship Messages Your team decides these items are needed: one leaflet describing the purposes and aims of stewardship – this to go to both groups; two action cards, one for each group; two envelopes – one a reply envelope for the action card, the other to enclose the whole kit of materials; a preprinted letter from your clergyman with handwritten salutation and signature. The Designer works out all the sizes and shapes so the Fixer can get printing/production estimates. The Chaser works out a timetable for the preparation stage and then one for the full timing through to the end of the campaign. The Reporter's task is to note the returned action cards and supply bulletins for church announcements throughout the campaign. He also liaises with the youth group leaders to ensure that the 17-21s are also enthused. Having persuaded a local office to part with an old card index cabinet for use in storing the action cards, the Forager now accepts the job of taking all those stewardship packs not picked up at the launch-service direct to the homes of church people.

The Writer drafts the main leaflet's text, taking care to think through both target audiences, whose circumstances will of course be fundamentally different. This copy explains the point your church has reached and what its needs and ambitions are; it describes the duties a church community has to God, to itself, to its locality, to specific groups of needy beyond; it helps the recipient discover the church's potential so that actions may be based on realistic aims; it stresses that the action card asks not only what people can do for the church, but also what the church can do for them. It includes a definition of Christian stewardship and the biblical basis for it – these same texts being delivered also from the pulpit. This flows naturally into a section on personal commitment, leading to items on Time, Talents and Resources.

Since this leaflet is the reference document, not only for the campaign's duration, but afterwards too, the Designer selects a card for printing which won't get dogeared too soon. On its cover a panel is left blank so that the recipient's name may be entered by hand. On the back is a timetable listing the church services and times during the campaign, along with clear deadlines for the making and confirming of commitments. The Designer selects a uniformly coloured paper stock to be used for all related print items, this to help people identify the stewardship activity rapidly. A rubber stamp is made so that the campaign title can be blazoned in red across the main kit envelope and on other items as necessary. Most of the text is typewritten in a big, open typeface so that recipients with poor eyesight will find it comfortable to read. For the same good reason the Writer keeps the wording short and plain so that the message in no way represents some crowded official form. The motif linking the church's name to the campaign title is drawn up and used on all items.

The action card is an A4 sheet concertina-folded into three panels, so it will easily fit the C6 return envelope. On its cover is a reprise of the stewardship appeal, asking that the Time and Talents sections be filled in and also the regular giving pledge on the reverse. Its first spread offers sets of tick-boxes, always in two columns. These are aligned with a range of activities under section headings: *Supporting Our Worship,*

Supporting Mission, Supporting Our Community, Teaching and Sharing, The Skills You Bring and *Your Own Suggestions*. The Writer takes care to be clear, noting such specific activities as 'hospital visiting', 'bell-ringing', 'welcoming new neighbours', 'helping with youth work', 'care of church linen', 'painting and decorating', 'artwork', 'Wednesday morning crêche', 'music skills' – and so on. The reader is asked to tick boxes in the first column if she already performs those tasks for the church and in the second if she would like to in the future. The text reassures her that no actual work commitment is made until further discussion takes place, where the details can be agreed realistically.

On the reverse are two sections. One is a list of services the church can offer the parishioner, with an invitation to tick such boxes as 'I would like to be visited', 'I need transport to church', and information requests such as 'put me on magazine circulation list', or 'send details on house groups' or 'tell me more about Confirmation'. Between that section and the one covering gift-pledging is a coupon for the recipient to complete name, address, telephone number details. The section on finance explains how regular giving makes the church's use of money more efficient. Covenanting is explained briefly. Your church already runs a pew envelope system; so a checklist of preferred giving methods is offered, including 'cash in weekly pew envelopes', 'monthly banker's order', or 'tithes'. There then follows a boldly displayed text which is headed *My Stewardship Commitment*, under which are a series of suggested payment amounts, each level indicated at weekly, monthly and quarterly rates, beginning at levels suitable for pensioners and rising through a range of increments, with a space left for the person to insert a figure of his own choosing. It is decided also to indicate also how much more these sums will be worth to the church when tax is recovered via the covenant system. It clearly states that no money should be sent at this stage. Finally, room is left for a signature or signatures.

While the printing is being done, the Cashier is busy briefing a team of 'converters' whose job it will be to take up action card pledges in conversation with the pledgers, seeing that pew envelopes are supplied, forms for banker's orders or covenants completed – and recording everything for the Chaser's files. The Chaser needs to note the level, method and frequency of giving agreed on his records so that, a year later, people can review it consciously.

Fundraising Activities

A clergyman does not come into the ministry expecting to be a salesman, nor does a congregation expect the profit motive to be a part of church life. The church is not a marketplace. It is a place of broadcasting, though, a centre from which Christians can turn outwards to face the world, sure in faith, clear in role. We must deal with that world, facing up to the part money plays in it. We shall not rehearse here all the well-aired Christian apprehensions about money – what it is the root of, what its pursuit distracts us from, or even where we cannot take it when we go – instead, let us say only that we have no need to be afraid of it. In short, if we are confident in the purposes to which we would put it, then we can be confident in the asking for it.

Good stewardship of the church resources and fabric, the spreading of God's Word, our response to the weak or needy – these things call for money as lungs call for air. If you don't have the money, you must set out to get it, and cheerfully. The Bible is direct on this matter, giving us (I Peter 4:10), 'Each one should use whatever gift he has received to serve others, faithfully administering God's grace in its various forms: And (Matthew 10:8), 'Freely you have received, freely give.' Your group's part in this is the provision of a channel, allowing a free passage for the latent but true desire to give, even among those who never have given – perhaps particularly among those. So, ask without apology. Receive in the manner of custodians, not beneficiaries. You will not have created a debt by asking, you will have allowed a repayment.

This natural soul-searching over, your team should find that raising money is quite simple.

Your main practical concern, as it is with all message-making, must be *to make a clean connection from the purpose, via the means, to the audience.* If you have a fixed audience and a fixed purpose for the fundraising, then your search is for the means – the event which will focus attention. If you have a fixed purpose and a fixed means, then your search is for the discovery of a matching audience. If you have a fixed audience and a fixed means, you need to find a purpose, a cause to fit them. Some examples follow.

A Means You have your church congregation (audience) and you have a damp west wall (cause); you need the means to release the giving of the first to solve the second. Solutions: you can take up a collection in church; you can launch a 'buy-a-brick' campaign; you can recruit a set of Saturday Squad volunteers whose one hour of work is worth £X, the potential giver having the choice of doing an hour's work or funding someone else to do it. (Note, in this last case, to take out temporary insurance against accident if your church policy does not cover 'amateurs' doing building work.)

An Audience You have a commitment to raise money for famine victims in Africa (cause) and plenty of literature provided by the charity on whose behalf you're collecting (means); you need to find an appropriate audience. Solutions: you can ask your youth group to take the appeal into their schools/colleges; you can take a team into local street markets (making sure they change collecting positions often to avoid antagonising traders – and gaining permission from the market authority first); you can challenge local restaurants to allow a collector among the tables once an evening – or agree with the waiters that they will split their tips 50:50 for a short period, you providing a leaflet explaining the deal to each donating diner.

A Purpose You have a fixed audience – the annual district fair on the green, and you have a fixed means – a stall allocated to your church; you need to find a purpose (cause) that matches the mood of the time and place. You have no shortage of purposes, but which might best catch attention? Solutions: knowing that many young families will be attending, you could set out to raise money for church crèche equipment, selling balloons overprinted with a message, this offered as a competition with a name and address tag tied to each balloon along with a request that its finder should contact the church, the eventual winner the one whose lighter-than-air balloon travels farthest, and the prize something suitable for a child; you can give the stall over to one of your church's teenage groups, who might set up a challenge competition based on sporting skill, contestants paying for a go to take on your group's champion, the prize being a free meal on club night, this raising money and potentially recruiting new members; you might run an auction of donated items, proceeds going towards providing the local retirement home with help or facilities, here taking care to make the auction proceeds as novel as possible – bidding coming, perhaps, in kind rather than cash (in rounds of sandwiches to be provided for an over-70s tea, or in units of half-hour visiting sessions designed to relieve loneliness among the elderly).

As this demonstrates, once purpose, means and audience are neatly connected, the fundraising becomes attractive and therefore effective, and fun to do. Triggering the impulse to give to something not previously in the givers' minds is entirely a matter of timing, appropriateness and 'understand-ability'. If you make the potential donor struggle to identify with your cause, you've lost the day in a second. Giving must seem obviously right in the moment of decision. If the donor gets a small reward in terms of novelty, entertainment or satisfaction, give it gladly for we cannot know at what point the greater awakening of faith may begin for that person.

The Language of Fundraising becomes a dialogue only

when the purpose/means/audience formula is complete. The seriousness or the lightness of tone, the 'pitching' of the message to tune it to the chosen audience's likely interests or educational level, the degree of moral justification according to the chosen purpose – all these choices must align with the formula, not be creative whims awkwardly tied on.

Having said that, a philosophical, abstract presentation rarely outdoes a vivid, plain one in that first moment of fund-raising encounter. Do not flinch from the propositional, concrete approach, for when people give on impulse, they almost always give to achieve a concrete result. At worst, the asker simply goes away, at which times the giving is starved of any value, cash or moral. At best, there is an implicitly good proposition. There is this need, you give now, we will then see to it that your gift meets that need. From this it follows that in the very presentation of the request must be the seed of the solution. 'Give to Africa' is not as concrete as 'Fight the Famine'; and in turn that is not as good as 'Stop Them Starving in Africa'. The closer your imagery approaches the point of alleviation in human and material terms – be it cure, revelation or practical provision – the easier it is for the giver to give.

Scale of Giving Imagine a range of giving all the way from the 10p-in-the-tin collection to the major corporate bequest and you will appreciate that a timescale must also apply. There is the 'one-off' giving stimulated by a specific event, and the 'structural' approach, where a person's giving extends over a longer period, perhaps promised ahead of time, even coven-anted. The relationship between one-off and structural giving needs to be understood by your group. Donors who give sporadically will include some who may graduate to com-mitted giving. Of these, some will sign something, being natural 'joiners', others will be ready to give often if asked often. The majority of impulse-givers will remain so, making it essential that your team knows the difference. Do not push such people to commit too hard; if they become defensive, back away. Do not hesitate, however, to ask committed, regular givers to give for occasional causes, for they will always be your best resource and will not react against your asking just as long as your church is seen to be also approaching a wider group of potential donors.

Take special care to review the money-gathering systems your church may already operate, avoiding the danger of allowing the subject of giving to become closed. It must be kept a 'live' subject, to the extent that everything from pew envelopes to the collection plate should be periodically rethought.

Your message-makers might like to consider a direct mail campaign, preparing, say, a bi-monthly appeal to the parish at large, using a rich and varied diet of subjects – some domestic (church repairs), some social (shopping scheme for the elderly), some overseas (orphans in India), some evangelistic (spiritual help for the middle-aged unemployed). Care must of course be taken not to duplicate elements of such a programme of appeals with existing funds of the church – a donor who has made a major grant to the renovation of the whole church building may feel you have been ignoring the gift if you also ask for money for a new door. Keep careful records of when, for what and how much a person has given. (See p 12 above about data protection.) After a time, it will become clear which subjects and which mailing treatments produced the best results. Do not concentrate solely on the top-earning appeal subjects without first considering how the pattern of appeals may have refreshed people's interest.

When asking for cash, try if you can to offer an ascending scale of suggested sums, probably three in all, ideally with each sum representing a precise response to need (£5 buys a yard of tiles, £15 buys an hour of a roofer's time, £50 buys x feet of guttering, etc). Here again, the experience of operating and keeping records of response will help establish the levels of giving people can afford, and the examples of amounts that seem to work best. It is as silly to underprice as it is to over-price. People are well used to dealing with money and will seldom prove as sensitive as you may fear – unless *you* make your appeal insensitively. People totally failing to respond to a succession of different appeals should be removed from that mailing list, though not necessarily off all lists. Try always to address letters to names, not to *Dear Member*. Ask your people to hand-write the envelope if possible, and if you are posting, stick a stamp rather than franking a batch of them. A letter from your church should seem personal.

Tin-rattling and Sponsorship Street collections need to be cleared with the local police and to be publicised in advance – a few days ahead will do. As a courtesy, be sure that no national street collection appeal is going to run at the same time as yours. The Charity Commissioners will tell you where a current annual list can be found. It is hugely more effective when the clothing or dramatisation of the collectors themselves is strongly related to the subject of the appeal. The public has an inate sense of what is fitting, a lively, amusing presentation being quite acceptable where the subject itself is not distressing – deprivation or death, for example. One church was successful with a roof restoration appeal having equipped its collectors with umbrellas painted all over with tiles, some of which were cracked or missing.

Sponsored-events have long been a feature of the Western scene, since bizarre activity usually draws attention from the local media. Here, take care to keep the theme of the presentation directly relevant to the purpose of the appeal. Doing a sponsored marathon walk in aid of Sudanese refugees is good; holding a gala dinner may not be. Find a title that communicates clearly even when spoken through a letterbox to a hard-of-hearing pensioner who is really more interested in eating his pudding. And when your team goes from door to door recruiting sponsors, not only should each sponsor be given a clear idea of the maximum performance possible by the person he is sponsoring – the most miles, the most lengths of the pool, or the fastest time, but he must also know what the related level of giving could add up to *at most* – i.e., 10 miles @ 10p a mile = £1. The equation does not stop there,

81

of course. It should be explained along these lines: 10 miles @ 10p=£1=3 days of dry ration for a Sudanese refugee child.

Give those who are enlisting sponsors official identification as bona fide representatives of your church. Tell them to enter a house only if they are personally known to the householder. When elderly people open their doors without first checking who you are – especially in cities – gently remind them to keep their door chains on for safety's sake.

Afterwards, once the sponsored participant's achievement has been officially validated, the collector should take along some kind of certificate as proof when collecting the pledged amount. If possible, try to leave a typed sheet summarising the outcome of the event, with an assessment of what good will be done with the sum so raised. If you satisfy and involve your sponsors *this* time, *next* time they'll oblige again.

A whole gamut of fundraising events is open to your group: from Hunt Balls to Third World Rice Dinners, from Passion Plays to Musical Talent Competitions. It must be said that as money-raisers these can be risky, depending as they do on a true entrepreneurial spirit in your team, a very well-judged audience and some realistic arithmetic. Such 'glitterati' events as might form part of somebody's social season lie outside the 'shoestring' brief of this book because they require a heavy cash investment before they can happen at all. Entertainment events can be based on experience or talents that most people – or at least some people – have within your group. The same is true for the perennials such as Fetes, Bazaars, Jumble or Bring-and-Buy sales.

To this last category of home-made, low-cost fundraisers, only two suggestions need asking. One, have someone who will specialise in pricing items realistically. Nervous *under*-pricing is not really a charitable act, it is a diminution of the cost and effort and quality that people put in free. *Over*-pricing tends to leave you with stock on your hands. Two, watch out for itinerant dealers in the first ten minutes of any sale: they are at best locusts and at worst can work in teams to distract the servers, bundling items into bags without paying for everything. The best defence here is to hold back some of your better stock for fifteen minutes, or till the first wave has passed.

Raising a Budget, again. On page 10, it is pointed out that the difference between subsistence and growth for any church, lies partly in its ability to raise funds. Year by year this will be seen as a seasonal chore by all save those fortunate foundations or orders with old investments yielding regular income. Between those and the minimalists who say 'The Lord will provide' and do nothing much to help him, the rest of us must come to an accommodation. Is the very precariousness of the church's income in itself a call to faith and effort? Once the church hall land has been sold off in exchange for a conversion to the church building, now too large alas for the remaining congregation, what assets are left? The answer is, only the present and future generations of a family holding, and a vision. Those are sufficient.

Your message-makers can help carry that vision and take care to pass on the knowledge of how it was done. Bring in others and multiply your new found skills, particularly with younger people. Try to work to plans longer than a single year and look for ways to consolidate vital income sources. Be ready, though, to exchange that comfortable certainty for challenging uncertainty if the Lord wills.

Department of Bright Ideas

The making of messages on a shoestring is often a process of using imagination as a cash-substitute. This is not such a bad discipline for communicators of all kinds, but with your church's slender means, ideas need to be absolutely practical, as well as imaginative. It is for that reason the advice offered here has been directed to individuals without ambitions as specialists, but with the motivation to help the work of their church to grow. They need ideas that are practical as well as bright. All 50 of the ideas that follow have been proven in practice, many of them drawn from responses to a survey among British churches carried out in the preparation of this book[1]. Most are small insights or techniques showing often that Christian message-makers can be serious without being dull, lively without being flippant, and that every new encounter is an opportunity to awaken response. One good idea leads to another!

Pavement Stencils

If you've a crazy inventor on your team, this gadget is for his attention. As part of its launch promotion a local weekly paper, which was to start coming out daily, publicised itself all over town by printing its name on the pavements. A push-along device based on the line-markers used to outline football pitches was adapted. To print, the advertisers cut away areas of a bristly doormat by half an inch, leaving the original top surface as a reversed left-to-right image for printing. The back of the mat was soaked with water. By means of a primitive camshaft the mat was alternately raised, then dropped into contact with the pavement, where it would leave a perfect imprint of a word, an arrow, footprints – anything. As the sun dries away the image after a while, no local ordinance is broken. A team of youngsters will do this all day long for you, and enjoy it.

Piggybacking

Are you on good terms with your local newsagents? If they are friendly, you may occasionally ask them to add a batch of your messages into their door-to-door deliveries. The principle is this: If you have a defined audience of, say, young mothers, or of males interested in sport, simply define which magazines such groups read, discover the delivery day for these, then arrive early at the newsagents to insert your message in the appropriate place in the newsboy's delivery

1 Except where a 'composite' version of an idea from many sources is given, such items are credited to the church concerned, with grateful thanks.

sack. In this way you have ensured it will reach an interested audience. It might only cost you a free mention on the small advertisement page of your church newsletter to persuade some newsagents. The same technique works even better with local bookshops, but here you should restrict your message to a small slip of paper, perhaps made to look like a bookmark. Book store owners have been known to allow this in return for some free help at stock-taking time. Your team goes in with some message bookmarks (one in yellow for young wives, one in blue for youth club potential members — and so on), and slips the appropriate ones into book titles that should attract the appropriate audiences.

Mobilise the Grapevine

When planning an event which offers some novelty or involves a celebrity, send out a team to 'talk it up'. Have them release small parts at a time by chatting in queues, at the school gates, over the garden wall. Orchestrate these 're-leases' so that a little mystery clings and local buzz builds up. The climax to a grapevine campaign should come just as the printed messages are displayed or delivered. Children are naturally good at this.

Talking Tins

When out collecting for an appeal in a public place, merely rattling a tin will not produce the desired result. Rattle your tin on a 'Come to me and put your money in' basis and you will be ignored by all but the positive – some might say conpulsive – givers. If you corner people and rattle it under their noses you will mostly be raising blackmail money and creating resentment. Tin carriers should certainly stand in the flow of people and by all means rattle, but they must also advertise what it is they want in short, clear, emotive and loud sentences, such as, 'Fifty pence feeds a child for a week.' Alternatively, have one or two people 'riding point' – spaced a dozen yards upstream and downstream of you, holding up posters and calling out the meesage. This allows potential givers to hear the fact that there is a collection coming up, that it is something they wish to support, to get money out of their pockets or purses and still be ready to put it into the tin by the time they draw level. This sensible procedure literally triples the collection.

Better Letterboxing

When leafletting, plan from the smallest letterbox up. Fold the printed sheet to pass through the smallest aperture without damage, so that it reaches the inside of the house with its key message showing. Even better, plan the design so that whichever way up the piece is handled by the house-holder, a key message bearing the essence of the proposition is readily seen. People give mere seconds of attention to unsolicited mail and only a glance at leaflets that come without envelopes. Think of someone getting an unexpected message from your church. Is the idea going to communicate itself fast? Does it encourage them to keep it and act on it?

Delivery Drill

Unless you wish the people inside to come to the door, do not clatter the letterbox loudly. Do close the gate after you without stumbling over the milk bottles. Do not leave the premises hurriedly as if leaving the scene of some crime. Know what is in the leaflet; if someone intercepts you and asks what it is, willingly explain it – person-to-person is your best chance of making someone co-operate with your purpose. Discourage

86

young leafleteers from hopping over neighbouring walls to save walking the long way round since this offends people. Don't take the dog with you. In estates or areas of terraced housing your dog can provoke a chain reaction of defensive howls and barks from house-dogs all along the way.

Understanding the Natives

Where your local dialect is full of images that may be bewildering to newcomers just moving in from out of the area, consider the example of Murdishaw Church, Liverpool, In a handy guide such jewels as these were explained: 'BLIND SCOUSE – a meat stew without meat, eaten in the interval between when the housekeeping runs out and the giro is due. THE WRECK – the local recreation centre'. Not vital information, but human and warm.

Prayer Adoption

This is where one person literally adopts another's problem in order to pray for its solution. A mother wanting her baby's recovery committed to God, fills in a simple prayer sheet – or multiples of it if she wishes to have more people praying, while people willing to offer intercessional prayer self-address envelopes marked Prayer Adoption. After a church service, those offering to pray reclaim their envelopes into which, by that time, a prayer request has been placed and sealed. The requester may remain anonymous or give as much detail as she wishes.. This encourages caring without building a false sense of debt or allowing condescension.

Nursing Home Service

The vicar of South Leverton Parish runs a spiritual and social service for patients on short or long stay in the local nursing home. The leaflet given to each person offers to make contact on his behalf with the clergy-man from his home parish; it offers visits by local people as well as private spiritual counsel; it offers to arrange attendance by clergy from some other denomination if that is preferred. It lists times of regular ser-

87

vices in the nursing home and prints a selection of helpful prayers for different circumstances: 'When in Pain', 'When Sleepless', 'Thanksgiving' and others. Although most churches offer some such visiting arrangement, this is a good reminder that not only practising Christians, but lapsed or curious people may need this encouragement.

Church Magazine as Visiting Card

The rector of St Michael's, Oulton, uses his regular parish newsheet in this way. Consider an extension of this idea, where a personal note might be added to a sticker placed on the cover. Magazine distributors could jot a word or two and a signature. The message could refer to an item inside or highlight a forthcoming activity. Such personal messages always get read and strengthen the contact.

Selling the Service

Barnsley Baptist Church put out some interesting leaflets aiming at a wider audience than the regular churchgoers. The principle is 'Be Our Guest'. When arranging significant services, consider extending the invitation list. It seems that double weddings or special baptisms and the like will bring in the shy 'outsider' who feels secure in the church environment, knowing he won't be the centre of attention while such events are going on. For such enquirers it means an opportunity to become familiar with the atmosphere, perhaps allowing the Spirit to work where even well-meant approaches by us might prove off-putting.

Paper Chase

St Augustine's, Bromley Common, turned newspaper into banknotes by organising a scrap collection. A giant skip was sited in the church car park on three well publicised occasions. Bundled newspapers or magazines and cardboard were dumped in it by parishioners. They reckoned to fill a skip with ten tons of paper over four days. Check who buys bulk paper in your district, what is the current price per ton and whether they will place and collect the skip.

Ditto Aluminium Cans

It is possible to negotiate approximately one penny per can. Some metal dealers require them flattened and sorted, providing a smashing evening for a youth group.

Church Postbox at Christmas

Rather than pay the standard postal rate, fix a lower rate for local delivery only by a church team. This can raise good revenue and spread your good connections. By selling Nativity stickers as stamps you can command perhaps 10p per letter. Operated purely as an internal arrangement between church members, this need not be regarded as a threat to the postal authorities. If your congregation chooses to buy Nativity stamps, with the proceeds going to a local children's home, and some other kind-hearted members offer to deliver some private communications for no profit, who could fault that?

Faith Aflame

The East Midlands Province of the United Reformed Church offers for 60p a pack of single-fold, four-page leaflets printed on various coloured papers, each addressing an aspect of coming to the faith. They develop the URC *Affirmation of Faith* and carry short, simple explanations, all reproduced from typewritten texts, entitled 'Faith Aflame'. This inexpensive presentation is kept neatly together as a set with a transparent plastic sleeve, the size suitable for an inside pocket or a handbag. The easily-understood, step-by-step way of presenting a complex and emotional subject may well influence new believers more than a bound volume.

A Legend in Your Lunchtime

Parishes located in busy urban centres, particularly office districts, might consider the initiative of Broadmead Church, Bristol. They offer their lounge room, called The Undercroft, for the use of local stores' personnel, office workers and city centre visitors for anything from a few snatched moments over a sandwich to more formalised gatherings. It is run by several groups of volunteers, some church people, some local workers. A worship area upstairs is available for 'City Prayers' or 'City

Communion'. Even if you do not own a property situated ideally for such an enterprise, remember that for years Oxfam and some other charities have 'borrowed' central store premises between lease sales or major reconstruction plans. Often for peppercorn rents a commercial firm will happily allow a trustworthy non-profit organisation use of the unemployed space. knowing it will be kept dry and not be vandalised, and well aware of the local public relations value of such lettings.

Untapped Talents

An interesting approach to increasing your church's pool of skills is to involve particularly those who are housewives, mothers, retired or between jobs. Almost all of these groups, while they may not feel deep discontentment, will probably feel to some degree under-used. Offer them a 'Talent Audit', listing more fully than would be usual for, say, a stewardship campaign, a review of options under headings like Administration, Education, Uniformed Groups, Young People's/ Children's Groups, Financial – and so on through into all the social and church-life categories. The Moortown Baptist Church, which does this more exhaustively than most, lists 153 options against which sit four tick-boxes. A tick in box 1 indicates past experience in that field; in box 2 a present involvement; in box 3 an interest in a future involvement; in box 4 a desire to receive training in that subject or activity. Simply by completing the list one person can better understand his feelings and motivations. Embark on such a survey only if your church is ready to act for these people, letting them release their talent through meaningful church-centred work. Indeed, the survey should be a challenge to your basic thinking.

Members' Address List

Churches with access to small business computers with good memory and print-out capability can consider putting their full list of members' names, addresses, occupations and telephone numbers on record. As updating is simple with computers, producing accurate current sets is simple. By photocopying the alphabetically-listed printout sheets and stapling them to a pre-printed card cover, a fresh church directory is quickly made available. These can be sold (at St Thomas' Church in Sheffield does so) for as little as 40p a copy, provided they are registered under the Data Protection Act. Consider also selling 'computer line ads' to local traders and make a profit on the venture.

An Unusual Leaflet-fold

A wide sheet of card which is cut at an angle across the top edge will, when concertina-folded allow you to display headings like this:

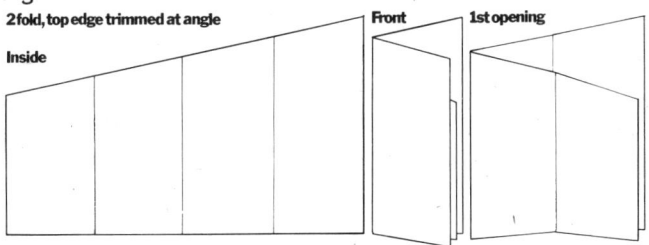

It is virtually impossible to resist looking through each section, making it ideal for the presentation of material of a categorised nature.

Insert Christmas/Easter Cards

If your church prepares a regular magazine, the inside pages of which are typed and duplicated, slipped inside a preprinted cover and then folded or stapled, you might consider this simple opportunity. Assuming that the finished size of the magazine is A5 upright, a greeting card may be prepared 8.5cm deep × 14.5cm wide (a wide shape) which, when folded, may be inserted between the covers and the inside pages prior to stapling the whole magazine together. This provides the following effect: Upon opening the cover, the face design of the card is overlaying the first right-hand page of text; the card's right-hand inside page, with its message and signatures, is encountered at the inside back page of the magazine. As its depth allows it to slip between the two staples, the card can be pulled out complete to join other greetings on the mantlepiece.

Public Speaking Competition

The Annunciation Catholic Youth Centre at Burnt Oak, Middlesex, runs a challenge trophy open to six teams drawn from local schools and clubs. Quite how you would choose to position your version of such an event would depend on the purpose you had in mind. It can become a way of drawing into your church young people with something to say. You may choose to formalise the event into a debate. You might like to take teams of mixed ages, say from 11-17, matching age for age in the competition, with team points being won all the way through. Your Forager could persuade local businesses to offer prizes for aspects of speaking performance – the most original, the most moving, etc. You could well choose to use it as an opportunity to ventilate pressing local social welfare issues, giving the whole thing a moral framework and getting the local media to cover it – perhaps publishing the winning speech. A local radio station, might be interested in a broadcast. In any event, run each speech to strict, short time limits.

A Couple of Don'ts among All the Do's

The typewriter has done vital service in rendering the handwriting of clergymen legible. The portable manual typewriter of long service is an almost sanctified feature of churches' printed materials. Its part in any duplicated sheet may be instantly recognised by its blotty, black, filled-in letters. While nothing short of new funds can save you from the quirky jumps in alignment and battered keys inevitable in an antique machine, regular cleaning will cure much of the filling-in. That was a Don't for the old school. Now here's one for the Space Age clergy replete with electronic word-processing equipment: stop showing off. Just because your machine can centre lines of text, be not led into the temptation of centring whole slabs of variable-length copy. The lines become tombstone-like inscriptions, and just as unlikely to be read. Avoid also your other inclination to justify margins on both left *and* right edges when the column width is very slim, All the poor machine can do in these cases is to put acres of space between words, producing a kind of typographical schizophrenia: one line of remotely spaced words, followed by another as congested as a traffic jam.

Counting the Pennies

Many a church treasurer has confronted the committee with the grinding logic of income and expenditure, only to find the conversation taking refuge in spiritual matters. Here are two aids to putting the case more arrestingly. You can calculate the weekly cost of running the church – survival essentials only – say a total of £186.30. You divide this by your total adult member or regular worshipper list, say 120 people. This produces a per member per week sum of £1.55. Compare this with your last year's averaged weekly offering, say £152.25, making a per member actual weekly gift of £1.27, a shortfall of 28p per person per week. At this point, committees tend to become moralistic and compare the 28p figure with the cost of a pint of milk or a daily newspaper, or whatever; the drawback with this kind of comparison is that it makes people defensive, not a good state of mind in which to encourage giving. Be positive. Rather than talk of recovering a loss (i.e. 'We failed last year'), talk of meeting challenge (i.e. 'Next year we must grow'). Think in terms of reaching out to people. In this light you will be discussing, not a 28p gap, but an ambitious growth in giving; not a survival level of £11.55, but an expansion to £2 per member minimum (accepting that those with greater means can volunteer to pay more, those genuinely hard pressed raising their present level by whatever they can manage). That is a positive presentation level by whatever they can manage). That is a positive presentation of the church's need, but it is still essentially a conservative approach. Try suggesting that every new member enlisted is a significant spreading of the giving load, quite apart from our Christian commission to bring others to Jesus. As suggested in the advance on stewardship campaigning (pages 66-68), you should help your people get the money issue into a positive perspective. You are not begging, but receiving on the giver's behalf; the use of the money is not for the gratification of individuals in the church, but for the service of God.

A Communications Conundrum

The simple first step in solving any communications problem – as explained earlier – is to 'line up' the audience, the means, and the purpose. Once those elements are truly inter-related, you make the message and communicate it. Once all those elements are right, don't be coy with a teasing presentation of the idea, don't edge up to the subject – just say it. And yet ... classical though this undoubtedly is, one letter from one clergyman, received in answer to our survey, comes as a timely reminder that, if an idea is so outstandingly unorthodox, it can succeed in spite of breaking the rules. In this case it was not an original idea – more a muddle – which is why no name will be mentioned here. In an envelope came a church newsletter and an unremarkable 'Time and Talents' appeal. This came out of the envelope first and caused an impression, not because of *its* impact, but because of the expectation the envelope had already aroused. This envelope, on closer inspection, turned out to have been re-used by the sender, having originated from Rentokil, whose logotype was printed on it, along with a sinister illustration of a beetle, captioned 'This'll bring the roof down.' In this sequence of miscommunication, the envelope's underlying message to the reader was, 'Look out, here comes a big appeal for the church roof restoration.' Upon encountering an altogether less dramatic or demanding appeal, the reader is put at once into a relieved, co-operative mood. When you use words and pictorial images, expectations are created, a dynamic which in itself can create results.

City Harvest

From the pages of the Battersea Central Mission (Methodist) magazine came an item headed 'We Plough the Streets'. It looked at the town-dwellers' version of Harvest Festival, suggesting that it comprised not 'fruit, flowers, vegetables and grain brought in from the fields and gardens' ... but a 'Preponderance of tins and packets ... more like a festival of St Michael's and St Sainsbury's.' In city parishes next October, why not consider a novel presentation of the harvest theme? What is the city's harvest if it is not agricultural? Is it the growth of understanding between ethnic groups? The saving of youngsters from drugs and crime? The harvest of new Christians? There must be more than enough drama here for a powerful event, a real challenge to the community as well as a thanks-giving. After all, by far the greatest part of the Western population is now city-dwelling.

Reunion Time

After the Mission England rallies around the country, individual churches were left to take up the names of local people who attended and came forward. The individuals referred to the churches had experienced the shock of Christian conversion, or the happy emotion of a faith rekindled. Such newly-won convictions become harder to sustain once the temperature is back to normal and everyday life crashes back in. But reunions have enabled people to relive the experience through audio-visual shows at local churches. This leads to an interesting idea: what about those whose decision for Jesus Christ was long ago and may perhaps not have involved a single, dramatic, unforgettable moment of conversion? Could your group create a drama event or a context for an exchange of experiences? It might be held in the late evening in a quiet church, associated perhaps with such powerful calls to commitment as the Good Friday or Christmas Eve vigils. Consider inviting as observers some who are close to accepting the faith and let the experience be rich, using music or projected slide images to focus attention.

Slide Show

These days, what with video cassettes a slide projector begins to seem like an old-fashioned machine; yet it is an essentially controllable, creative tool, the essence of which is in the imagination *you* put in. A single projector on a single screen or white wall can be effective for such purposes as leading hymn singing or illustrating sermons; the use of two synchronised projectors gives you a more fluent show; the images from alternately-firing projectors merging smoothly into each other can almost simulate real motion, and may still be controlled frame by frame by a hand-held gadget. These units can be hired for special shows, though you need to leave plenty of rehearsal time to get the slide order exactly right; it is possible to use up to twelve – probably more – projectors, but that takes money and professional knowhow. You can borrow or buy a device which can make a pulsed sound tape which signals to the projectors precisely when to release their slide, allowing you fast or slow fades and any length of hold on any image. If you do not want the obtrusive presence of a voice speaking live as the slides change, you can record a voice-track onto the sound tape along with the pulse. Where you wish to use a slide-show for a travelling programme, this at least guarantees a consistency of presentation. At a simpler, person-controlled level, consider a *son et lumière* show, using the inside of your church as the projection area. Using a number of different projectors – all with long-throw lenses – and a variety of simplified images which can be painted directly onto clear glass slides with photo-opaque paint, you can make breathtaking dramatic effects in the darkened space, images appearing on ceilings and other flat surfaces. On the subject of projected images – consider also the humble overhead projector. It is also used for projecting hymn or chorus verses by some churches, yet with a little imagination it can make a wonderful shadow theatre, using silhouetted shapes and texts written onto acetates – marvellous for young children in Sunday School.

Pedal Round the Parishes

A sponsorship well worth adapting to your locale is this one run – perhaps we should say *ridden* – by members of St Margaret's, West Hoathly. The principle is to involve different denominations in a local circuit of churches. Rather than set strict time limits, the idea is to have as many churches to visit as possible. Each participating church can put up a team of riders and a team of signers-in. Each cyclist has a sheet with all the stages listed on one side and a good street map on the other – protected from weather and mishaps by a clear plastic sleeve. At each call, an official of that church signs and marks the time of arrival. According to how relaxed you wish the event to be you must decide whether to have miniature receptions at every church, though there should always be time for a prayer or a blessing, with perhaps two or three main half-hour stops for rest and refreshment at selected churches. Each rider is sponsored for a sum to be multiplied by how many churches he reaches. Teams of riders, handicapped according to age (fewer churches required to be visited if they're over 40/50/60), set off together, returning to their own finishing point – their own church – either having completed their fixed circuits, or when their legs will accept no further punishment. They are then 'signed out'. Should you want to introduce more competitive elements for, say, teenage riders, over-fifties, clergymen, etc, the opportunity is there – as is the chance of considerable local media coverage. If the numbers involved get above a couple of dozen – which they should – clear the date and the route plan with the police. This is a fine weather event. (Don't forget to insure!).

A Word about Word-of-Mouth

The size of the local population partly determines whether ambitious plans for church growth are achieved. Given reasonable numbers, the will and the energy, growth can happen. Some rural parishes have no such resource, serving only tiny hamlets. The Rev C Pattison of St Hedda's, Egton Bridge in Yorkshire has scarcely 130 parishioners. He occasionally goes into print with an old Banda carbon copier: 'It is not laborious to produce – a gallon of print spirit lasts a year – not messy to work with, and makes an imprint on cheap paper. I'm satisfied that it does the job to keep my congregation and pocket happy.' Rev Pattison is right not to feel defensive, as those running low-population parishes can truly take advantage of the best medium of communication there is – direct and unbroken human contact. Virtually all other message-making is an attempt to substitute for that relationship, the one that characterised Christ's ministry. It would not be a good idea, however, to let a small world be the only world. Urban and rural clergy and communicators have much that is useful to share: consider then a kind of 'twinning' where you might share experience, ideas and prayers, as detailed by Peter Elsom and David Porter in their book on employment called *Four Million Reasons to Care* (MARC, 1985).

Pew Notes

John da Costa, Vicar of St Mark's, Mansfield, is 'hot' on pew notes, saying there is a danger of 'Too much of the "Sound of the Wind in the Palm Trees", and not enough of Glory to God in the High Street.' Each pew note is written in an easy, intimate style, taking a topic and then challenging each family to take the note home for consideration after the service. The notes can be typed and cheaply duplicated on slips of paper. The congregation may be encouraged to circulate them more wisely by strategic placement in hairdressers' or dentists' waiting rooms, in friends' homes or at places of work. If they are written with warmth and accessibility, they become a good advertisement for worship at your church, the name and address of which – it is worth repeating – should be clearly indicated.

A Time for Vocation

A call to the ministry may come strong and early for some, almost imperceptibly and late for others. The idea of a Vocation Month is from the Rev R J Avent of St Augustine's, Kilburn, for which his church produces a thoughtful outline that takes a person through a self-examination, asking them to complete written statements using the guidance notes and a good deal of prayer; these personal evaluations are kept by the person to be read and privately reconsidered. All prompting is left to the individual, with the next practical steps made clear, the door to ordination held open. The beauty of this idea is that while it speaks to the person clearly drawn to the vocation, it has a message of awakening for others with potential but thus far little awareness.

Saying It with Flowers

From the same church a more extrovert expression of faith: a flower festival, with music. This idea is for an event of some scale, run over two or three days and intended to draw substantial audiences at £1-per-family tickets. On these days the church is garlanded with floral displays at every possible point, these supplied by individuals, local firms or social groups or by other neighbourhood churches. During the daytime, a series of one-hour organ recitals is given, entrance free but collection boxes handy. Each evening, a more formal concert is given, entrance by programme. Audiences can be drawn from congregations of all churches providing floral displays. Sponsorship expenses by local firms and individuals is essential; such sponsors will get complimentary tickets but also be asked to sell further tickets to staff and customers. Churches of other denominations will see that if they help you to stage a major event like this, they may ask for reciprocal co-operation later.

Trailers for the Seasons

Such is the habit-forming nature of the rotation of church seasons that a keen sense of anticipation is often absent from our experience. How to encourage this expectation? Answer: make 'trailers' for them. The priest at the Roman Catholic Church of St Thomas of Canterbury prepares a 'Focus' sheet for seasons such as Advent. In this he explains the meaning of Advent's three phases, giving advance notice of the readings for each service. He also provides a historical explanation of the pagan winter solstice tradition, along with a calendar of all associated events for the period.

'Consumer' Surveys

Several of our Christian traditions have in recent times undergone the convulsion of a revision to the form of service. After some soundings among the laity, such changes are approached primarily through dialogue and prayer at the higher levels of the Church. Issues of theology and church law apart – these things may not be negotiable – what does the worshipping community (the non-professionals) feel? Factors of local culture and social composition play a part, so that what is seen as vital by one group may not be vital for another of the same tradition in a nearby parish. How many assumptions can be made? Can the incumbent totally understand people's poorly articulated feelings here?

Consider a survey such as that circulated by the Hythe Methodist Church. Those completing questionnaires are free to sign or not sign them, as they choose. The idea behind the survey is to make public worship more meaningful by discovering where consensus might be found across a whole range of topics. The questionnaire form is designed for YES/NO ticked answers. It asks questions such as which versions of the Bible are preferred; whether readings are well done, and if they are best read by the clergy or by members of the congregation; whether the passages selected are well related to the sermon or address; whether certain books of the Bible are being neglected; whether non-biblical readings are acceptable; and whether Bible study is available in helpful forms? Similar questions are asked about the shape, presentation and placing of prayers, psalms and singing. The approach to and delivery of sermons is analysed, with questions on participation. The Eucharist/Communion and family Worship are similarly examined, with questions about length of time, the composition of the congregation and the desirability of variety in presentation. Finally, a list of options for service times is given. Care is taken to encourage criticism and praise within a framework of constructive analysis. This survey is brave, for it implies an intention to act on the findings.

Should You Go Electronic?

We cannot dismiss the looming possibility that future generations may never need to put pen to paper, that printed text will surrender to all kinds of electronic transmissions and computerised alternatives. Churches now comfortable with audio-visual aids are threatened with the kind of leap that once made the magic lantern show obsolete. Inevitably, church worship must be profoundly affected. The Christian church has for its entire history kept the handwritten or printed word at the centre of its message-making, and it is the written word that is under threat, not the spoken word. In some ways, despite an amazingly rapid communications revolution, our oral tradition is becoming our greatest strength. How may we prepare ourselves for the changes? First, if your clergy or leading laity is willing to come to grips with the electronic media, consider enrolling someone in a training course so that your church can be heard in this new age, or delegate someone to study more informally. Then, if your church wants to make its own programmes for video tape, discover now whether your own denomination's central body offers such facilities; and if not, ask a few sharp questions about the denomination's readiness for a generation which reads electronic images the way others have read books. One of the vanguard of new churchmen in this field is the Rev Lawrence Mortimer, vicar of St James', Styvechale, and Diocesan Broadcasting Officer. He transmits via Mercia Sound and chairs an inter-denominational broadcasting committee in the area. Contact: *Church of England Enquiry Centre,* 01-222 9011, Ext 264/265/266. Other useful contacts include *CTVC* (01-950 4426) Hillside, Merry Hill Rd, Bushey, Watford, Herts WD2 1DR, which offers training for Christian broadcasters in radio and TV; video, film and audio production facilities; and *Christian Broadcast Training Ltd* (0638 668491) Severals House, Bury Rd, Newmarket, Suffolk, CB8 7BS, which offers residential training for Christian broadcasters. For other, more specialised services and resources, see MARC Europe's publication *UK Christian Handbook.* In these two ways, rather than making reluctant concessions, your church will adapt thoughtfully and creatively.

Neighbourhood Visiting Scheme

To make visits to the elderly and housebound more successful, let them know of the scheme by dropping cards through their letterboxes inviting them, their friends or helpers, to make contact by telephone. Do as the Methodist Dawley Christian Centre people do – recognise that many of the folk they want to encourage will have poor eyesight, and print in large-type on brightly coloured card that they can keep by their telephone or bedside. Equip your troupe of visitors with large-print copies of the Old and New Testaments (if in doubt ask the Bible Society which supplies softback *Good News* versions published by the American Bible Society for use by preachers (0793 486381) Stonehill Green, Westlea, Swindon, Wilts SN5 7DG). Many older people miss reading the Bible and enjoy even more reading *with* someone. If you can afford it, attach to the invitation cards a photocopied picture of the visitor who would come; this introduces the visitor to shy or timid people and is a help in making sure the right person is welcomed into the home. It is not essential to match the visitor's age to that of an elderly housebound person, but in the case of disabled people do try to match ages and interests – such people are sensitive to being patronised – and a few careful questions early on can avoid mistakes. With the disabled, visitors can discuss ways of putting compatible housebound people in touch with one another.

Paper Weight

Consider bulk paper purchase – a worthwhile idea if your print requirements allow you to preprint an element – a colour nameplate or some design or symbol in colour so that, later, you can take the sheets from stock and overprint in black, giving a brighter effect with no loss of time. Only do this if you can plan efficiently and have sufficient storage space, free of damp or dust. If you are attracted to this kind of saving, involve the Designer in working out how large preprinted sheets could be guillotined by a printer into more than one useful stock size. Part of the planning here is to know how the paper is ultimately to be folded and to be sure that envelopes, where needed, will be of the right size. (See table of 'A' paper sizes on page 155).

'Personalised' Marriages

To the discomfort of their members, some churches use old, preprinted forms or service sheets that have become out of date and are therefore hand-corrected; these look a little scruffy but may be adequate for general services. For such purposes as weddings and funerals, though, the appearance of the materials is meaningful, and what may be no more than economy-mindedness can appear to be heartlessness. Those churches with access to word processors and disk storage can easily defend against outdated forms; they can print out each time an updated and accurate master for photocopying. The effort is small, each 'edition' being made personal to the families concerned, with the names of bride, groom, child for baptism, the deceased, or those to be confirmed included. Some progressive churches even print the names and addresses – even the rates – of suppliers like photographers or florists, charging them for ad-space, of course!

Do They Know They're in Your Parish?

As the church parish boundaries and those of the civic authority do not always coincide in location or name, one way to let newcomers and even longtime residents understand the discrepancy is to send them a parish map with their home and your church clearly indicated. Fr Peter Fell of St Begh's, Whitehaven, uses such a map in a leaflet as a prelude to a Survey Team visitation. The caller will be asking parishioners to indicate what they need from the church. One phrase used inside this leaflet, referring to the Church of Christ, is worth repeating: 'It is nineteen and a half centuries young. It will still be around in the year 2000, and 3000, and . . . Meanwhile, if we can be of any help to you . . .' That should help give Christians a sense of location!

103

Cashometer Graphic

Adapted freely from 'Across Exmoor' parish magazine comes a neat way to express your church's finances at a glance. We print it here sideways to save space. Feel free to photocopy it for your own use, with a prayer of thanks to the anonymous contributor.

The Message Is: Access

St Andrew's-with-Castle Gate (URC) runs an imaginative social service for broken families. Theirs is not the task of marriage counselling, but of facing up to the awful position where the parent *without* custody and without money can see his or her children only for fixed periods and is trapped in a circuit of cinema visits, walking the streets or local parks, none of which gives a real opportunity for relaxed contact. Families most in need are those where the ex-husband or ex-wife is either legally forbidden – or is not capable of – private meetings. A centre run by volunteers in teams of two is open all day every Saturday, with games for the children to play, plenty of space and plenty of privacy. If you like the idea, talk to your local social services department who will give you advice and probably refer to you some families needing help. You may also qualify for a grant towards equipment and costs. It is out of the bleakness of such situations that people can discover faith.

Prayphone

Variations of this idea exist across the country. In some parishes it is a service provided by a group of disabled people or retired folk; sometimes the service is available between fixed hours so that a whole group can gather by the telephone to offer concerted prayer. Typically, there is a Prayer Directory indexed by subjects so that a caller can be offered a prayer whose message exactly fits the circumstance. A more ambitious version has the prayers already tape-recorded against a musical background; here each prayer is coded according to its place on the audio-tape counter so that the prayer can be located and commence playing within seconds.

Dear Diary

This is what they call in America a 'freebie'. A church can order quantities of diaries at surprisingly reasonable cost for distribution as Christmas or New Year gifts to parishioners and new friends alike. Several printers produce a light, papercloth-cover, pocket-size diary, most of it already printed, allowing key pages for your church's own information. In addition to details of the church calendar, there can be other typical diary information from metric measurements to bank holiday dates. Most important: page spaces can be sold to local trades-people to offset the overall cost. One such diary is that of the Knowle URC, where the Minister, the Rev Graham Spicer, advises users to 'mark in some space for themselves, the better to enjoy the gift of being alive'.

Rate Card

Consider the example of St Matthew with St Barnabas, Hull, who have an A5 four-page leaflet designed for local advertisers. It is modelled on the commercial rate cards issued by magazine publishers and is of a format practical for any church to follow. The cover carries a slogan, the point of which is to underline the main benefit an advertiser could expect from using the monthly church magazine. This is followed by 150 words noting the numbers sold or circulated and the number of adult readers each issue will reach. It offers a choice of *classified* (wording only with advertisements under categories) or display (advertisements with text plus design). It points out that, for a matter of pence per month as many as 2000 people (in their case) can read about a local product or service. The magazine's title design is shown boldly here. It mentions discounts for series bookings (a minimum of six months booked in advance). The inside spread shows a collage of advertisements which ran the previous year, this to show advertisers that other products or services have been entrusted to the magazine. On the back is a list of prices per size, type and frequency of ad, along with a booking form. An alternative to the centre spread described above might be the use of testimonials by previously satisfied customers. Altogether a neat item, this rate card has an order and directness which strongly suggest the magazine itself will be equally effective.

In Praise of Classifieds

The Rev Allen Bagshawe of the above church gives another revenue-raising tip on the same topic. You can sell the back page of your magazine not just the once, but twelve times. How? Split it into two, putting the ad for 'Sponsor of the Month' in the top half while in the bottom half list the twelve months of the year along with each month's sponsor, his address and telephone number. The advertiser is therefore guaranteed a solus ad for one particular month and a linage ad for all twelve.

Colour Identification Works

Quite the best thought-out and executed programme of print materials sent in response to our survey was that by St Paul's, Hasland. Members there have linked a sequence of contact, conversion, and follow-up leaflets by the simple means of a colour scheme of brown on white, brown on fawn, and a strong graphic symbol of circular design carrying a Christian motif and the church's name. The stationery matches throughout, giving an effect of cohesion. Anyone receiving the first two items would instantly associate any later piece in the set with St Paul's. Their team had a vision of what

106

their messages should achieve over a period, and the result is simple and direct enough to work very well.

Matthew 25: 14-20

From St Paul's Methodist Church, Northgate, Crawley, comes a most biblical fundraiser. The treasurer there gave to each participant a brand new one pound coin, (51 in all). This cannot have been an easy thing for a church treasurer to do, but Martin Bower bravely did so! The principle is, of course, that – not wishing to be the servant who buried his talents rather than lose or multiply them – the participants would return, having at least doubled the value through activities as various as making jams or growing plants for sale, baby-sitting or house decorating.

What's Going on?

A simple A5, 44-page booklet arranged as an A–Z of the goings-on in the Northampton parish of St Gregory the Great (RC), typed, not type-set, duplicated, not printed—here is an example of how a simple idea can convey the character of a church and its community. Each page of the book has a single entry, starting with A for Abington Wind Band and ending, somewhat eccentrically, with . . . A for Addendum. Every item tells you the appropriate contact's name, when, where and why things happen, with hardly a page with more than 100 words on it. How much more readable and 'keepable' this is than are some of the crammed lists which try to present the same kind of material. The difference? It is full of humanity.

Stings in the Tail

Here, a small object lesson in balancing the delivery of a message. The first paragraph of text culled from an (anonymous) parish magazine reads: 'The Smiths, like others, have moved away. Some have vanished without trace. Others have fallen away. What this list means, is even though four people have joined the congregation, the annual return will show our church's membership lower than in

1985.' Believe it or not, this gloomy passage eventually led to a fairly optimistic challenge to recruit new members. You could forgive most readers, though, for having given up rather earlier, never to receive the point of the message. In contrast, here is a caption drawn from a church's Third World appeal leaflet. A fairly innocent looking TV set shows on-screen a pot of instant coffee marked ACME COFFEE. Out of the set's speaker issues a word bubble carrying this caption: 'To bring you coffee at the best possible price we've reached higher into the hills, where the workers are paid even less, where the housing is even more primitive.' Both messages leave the point to the end, yet the optimistic end-point of the first is wasted while the savage pay-off line of the second scores high marks by carrying the reader all the way. It always takes two to complete a communication.

One Sunday This Summer

Just once, hold the entire morning service out of doors. Sing, pray, preach and praise God, not in the familiar, safe territory of a building private to your church community, but out there in a park, on the Green, in a field or in the pedestrian area of the civic centre. Try dramatic sketches in the shopping centre, with permission from the police, or musical processions at Easter or Whitsun. See the effect on your people and on the world outside.

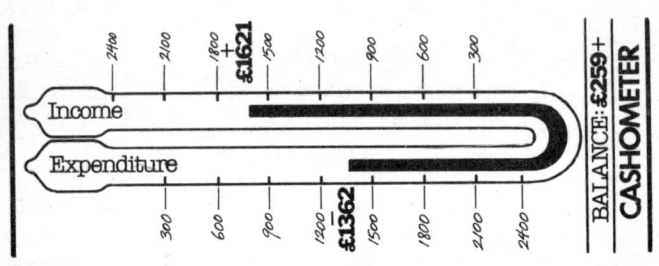

Part III
Doing

The making of a message is a practical affair, with the end product seldom revealing quite how much thought or difficulty lies behind it. Even so, some things are revealed. A muddle is a muddle for all to see and will consequently probably not be read or heeded. What any group can learn to do, long before any sophisticated skills develop through experience, is to eliminate muddled thinking. To do so, planning has to be clear, the approach has to be simple and your message must contain a single main challenge only. Let your team be clear. Being amateurs – doing it voluntarily – is admirable. Being amateurish – doing it without discipline – is silly.

What, then, may we reasonably expect from people who have no professional skills in this field, who give their time and talents free? We can expect a team who as Christians will ultimately put the importance of the challenge before personal pride. But we must also demand from the team Leader great sensitivity in dealing with the team. Make it clear that the early work is aiming for clarity, not elegance. After the first message will come confidence and less apprehension; a style will eventually flower that is totally your church's own.

Since each specialist must start somewhere, some technical advice is offered in this part, mainly for the Designer, but also for the Writer and the Reporter, whom we shall consider first. Even here the concentration is on the basics of the process, as it is vital that your church finds its own level of expression through ingenuity and imagination. Let the making of the message, the 'doing', be enjoyable in itself, a praise to God.

Doing the Writing

Perhaps the most difficult task for the Writer is to separate his

personal style from messages made on behalf of the group. As professional writing standards do not apply to most people's jobs, most of us develop styles which are amalgams of received ideas and particular work experience. A diplomat might adopt an 'arm's length' style, a lawyer a precise style, a salesperson a chatty style – and so on. Those who are ordained will have absorbed not only the substance of their religious training, but also a certain tone of voice. Indeed, there is a considerable jump in attitude required when moving from a direct delivery of God's Word, or some illumination of it, to a more mundane appeal for funds in aid of some earthly purpose. The authority of the first does not carry directly to the second, nor – it should be said – the second to the first.

The practical approach is for the Writer to detach himself from the subject, holding a mental picture on the one side of the chosen audience for the message – their level of interest, their ability to respond, their known attitudes – and on the other, a picture of the proposition the church is making. The Writer has only to find the most direct route between the two and the style will find its natural level. As long as this transaction is carried out in honour of God, whatever the actual subject, the writing will be good enough. With this responsible detachment and a concern for finding the right channel for each particular occasion, it will become evident whether a message needs to be formal or informal; how informative or demanding, how long or short it ought to be. This detached view is likewise necessary in the way your church's more long-term messages go out: a workable style has to seem consistent even in its most extreme applications.

Here are some guiding principles for the Writer, not overly concerned with the more particular aspects of grammar. Good grammar naturally aids understanding, but good grammar without a clear understanding of the reader's needs is useless.

Writing Principles

Write in terms of dialogue Except in necessarily formal cases, try to think of your audience as represented by one typical individual. Imagine what her levels of receptivity and vocabulary might be. Think how you might have to tackle the conversation face to face; think what objections or questions might arise. Then you will know how to express the written message.

Talk up to people, not down Communicating for a good cause can lure a Writer into an authoritative role, encouraging a master-and-pupil relationship from the Writer's viewpoint and probably no relationship at all from the audience's. Even without the good excuse, the well-educated often assume the teacher's role when addressing a less-literate audience, an assumption that does not take account of other, compenting abilities such as intuitive intelligence or 'street' wisdom. A reader knows when she is being patronised even when the Writer may be blithely unaware of it. Talk *to* them, not *at* them, and you've freed the path that carries the message to them.

Words are also pictures Christian message-makers are so imbued with spiritual concepts that they may weaken their writing with abstract expressions. Though these are real to the believing community whose faith and practice make them flesh, to most outside this circle, the images presented by words like 'grace' remain insubstantial. Messages dealing entirely in such terms pass most mortals by. Jesus used

111

comparative imagery to fix ideas and to stimulate deeper questioning in people's hearts (the shepherd, the vine, the highway robbery and the hated Samaritan). Concrete nouns summon up vivid images, engage a reader's interest and encourage action. Linking such images in sequence aids memory and encourages the 'ownership' of the ideas. To carry such images along use direct, active verbs, they put high energy into the colourful images. When the budget for your messages is too small to afford pictorial support, make your headline messages powerful in this way. For all their vulgarity and dubious content, the popular tabloids know how to do this; since the majority of our population reads them, a little thoughtful study might help!

Louder may not be clearer There is a send-up recording well known to the advertising industry, in which a group of company executives and agency men are in a studio to make a radio commercial for Blooper's Soap. The script is simple. It says 'Blooper's soap is good for you'. Each time the actor speaks the sentence into the microphone, one executive or another wants one of the words stressed – 'BLOOPER'S soap is good for you' – 'BLOOPER'S SOAP is good for you' – and so on until, predictably, the actor is shouting the entire sentence. The printed message is not so different. You simply cannot make everything seem important. Things need to be read in the order the Writer decides, and the various devices for giving emphasis – underlining, bigger or bolder or italicised passages or exclamation marks – all must be used sparingly. Even more important is to avoid peppering the text with those single words that suddenly jump up in capitals. That kind of frantic enthusiasm is too tiring to read and almost always betrays a Writer who speaks with profligate emphasis.

Demand one action only Give a reader one choice at a time. Asking someone to give money is one choice followed by another, related choice: He has the choice on *whether* he will give money; then he has the choice *how much* he will give.

112

In fact, the real decision is made once the person sees the need, for then the value of the gift, and his ability to pay it, both come into line. Do not therefore expect somebody to consider sending a cash gift, at the same time to supply the names of other potential donors – and to consider committing some time to your cause. You will have moved out of a simple transaction into some kind of survey, leaving the reader confused, hesitant over the second and third propositions, possibly having decided 'yes' to the first. He will not have to reject the ideas, but he only has to defer the decision and you have lost the opportunity, perhaps for ever. If those other propositions are so essential, make separate events of them.

Read your text out loud Its faults will be revealed.

Use fewer words Bernard Shaw once wrote in a letter that he would have sent a postcard, except the shorter message would have taken him longer. Take the time to write the message in fewer, more potent words. After all, anyone encountering an unsolicited message has first to decide whether or not to *start* reading it. Long grey passages are where people do not choose to walk. Is your material saying, 'Don't read me'? Write fewer words; group them in compact sentences.

Write captions to pictures It has been proved that people will often read a caption while ignoring a headline. This suggests that the caption might be used to repeat the key message of the headline. Certainly avoid the trap of saying in the caption what any halfway intelligent person could perfectly well deduce from the picture, unaided. Use the caption to add information.

Know how much information is enough Think through the detail of your message and be sure that you are making no untrue assumptions as to how much background the readers already understand. Equally, do not bother them with repetitions of what they do know. Above all, do not use 'inner circle' references to subjects unknown to the wider audience, or pat phrases that mean something only to the favoured few: 'I've got a burden for so-and-so'; 'You'll get a blessing from this word'; 'He's been saved.' All these exclude your audience and deprive them of the very truth you want to convey.

Position your relationship From message to message, from subject to subject, there will be variations in tone, treatment and content. Yet try to establish across the range of your church's materials a consistent stance in relation to the readers. Are you going to be a little distant: 'The church will be holding a Talent Auction on June 2nd', or be an identifiable human unit, still at a slight distance: 'The Friends of St Cuthbert's invite you to . . .', or an almost neighbourly proximity: 'We invite you to our Talent Auction . . .', or the one-to-one intimacy: 'Come and buy the talents I'm auctioning on . . .'? There really are no fast rules here. Find a position and stay with it.

Check the structure of your message In any request for a response, be sure you have the anatomy right. These phases must be present – usually in this order: catching the attention, making the challenge, amplifying that challenge, calling for response. Rarely can you propel the reader from the first two to the last. Sometimes you can simultaneously present the first two. But play safe and keep all four in place. People have learnt to deal with propositions; they want all their reservations dealt with before they can say 'yes'.

The reader must first recognise the existence of the message – an action repeated dozens of times a day – but the contact will be broken if some element of the proposition does not hook a deeper attention. It is well-attested that the reader's next instinct is to check who is making the proposition. An offer of 'sun, sand and sea' may be less attractive if the country offering it is in the middle of a border dispute. The reader is asking, 'Is this relevant or irrelevant to my life?' Then, if it is, 'Does it come from people I trust?' If you've failed to get instantaneous approval at either stage, you've lost the person. If you still have him, he will read supporting text. This tells you that using the attention-getting device headline to tease the reader can be counter-productive, and that you should do so only if the device is outstandingly strong. The point is that you want the reader to do something; but even if he is interested, he will con-sider what benefit the church is offering in return. The text has to move the reader through this question, though of course the benefit need not always be material. A free product trial is not so very different from an invitation to a new neighbour to try a service at your church. Even where the person is spiritually motivated to accept an invitation of the sort offered, he still has to answer the question 'Why *this* church?' Sometimes familiarity flavours such apparently non-propositional news announcements as: 'Fancy Dress Ball this Saturday'; you have the advantage that, knowing how much fun your previous events have been and knowing very well what a fancy dress ball is like, the reader will want to take the opportunity offered. Normally though, a proposition needs to be added; 'Help the disabled' written above a picture of a group of static, seated people does not quite work as a proposition, somehow; while the optimistic 'Six wheelchairs by Spring' suggests a solution to an implicit problem, an understandable and *achievable* target for giving. You assume a latent interest in the reader, and already he is reading the text or jumping ahead to the bottom of the message to see what kind of action or sum of money is expected of him.

The reader demands more than an expansion of infor-mation as he reads, because he is looking for encouragement to complete an action already suggested to him, one which he finds attractive. A sudden dissection of the pros and cons will not help, nor will an interesting aside on a tangential topic. The route between the challenge and the requested action must be as direct and uncluttered as possible. The supporting points in the text should be so simple and clear that the reader can adopt them as arguments in favour when he uses them in discussion with another person.

When asking for response of any kind, believing as you do in the value of what you ask, do not be tentative. Not only will this convey uncertainty, it also underestimates people's generosity. Whether you are asking for effort, advice, prayer support or cash, see it not as taking a liberty but as rendering a service, and ask boldly.

Make it easy to read There is good sense in the standard advice to public speakers, 'Tell them what you are going to say, say it, then remind them what you just said.' In long passages of printed text and short paragraphs alike, this holds true. The fact is that, unlike readers of newspapers who have *chosen* to read them by paying cash, the readers of unsolicited messages cannot be expected to give the same automatic attention. Even so, newspapers go to great lengths to attract and sustain high readership. Each topic is signalled, often with a spicy or intriguing headline; columns of text are broken up with short subheadings designed to keep the flow of attention going and give an outline picture of the story's content. Why should newspapers do that? Rarely do people relish total surprises, but they do adore the frisson of informed anticipation. Let your longer texts adopt this technique.

Let people into the text In an essay a paragraph is the container for a complete thought. In writing messages, this structure becomes a luxury if long sections remain forbidding and unwelcoming. The editorial technique noted above can help, as can some good typography. Get your Designer to make three-space indents at the start of sentences and contrive to write shorter paragraphs so that there are plenty of them. Those small inlets of space at the beginning and end of a paragraph actually encourage reading.

Big numbers don't count Very occasionally impressive

116

statistics may lend weight to a disaster appeal or to build the potential of some new Christian initiative in people's minds. To say that a national campaign target is for a million people to hear the Good News is perhaps helpful in establishing the importance of an event prior to asking one individual to become involved; for that one person, though, the figure of one million has no shape. Big numbers may arrest attention, but they seldom win an argument or a convert. For that campaign it would be better by far to say, 'Our town has a target of one thousand,' or better still to say, 'Our church has a target of one hundred.' Best of all say, 'Our team has a target of nine a month.'

The same holds for other information. A general idea is remote, but a particular idea is personal. It is all a question of where you start. Christians know very well to start with the individual and to bring that life into the fuller context by degrees. The big numbers have a place: use them to reinforce truths the reader has already experienced.

Read the principles addressed to the Designer

Technical Information

Plain intelligence must be the Writer's main tool, though the lack of a typewriter can cause difficulties. You must try to get all materials meant for your group's messages into consistent, legible form, and a typewritten text is safer than handwriting. Agree in the group that all copy for printing or any other kind of reproduction or broadcast should be typed on a distinctive coloured paper, and that colour will not be used for any other communications; that way, text is always identifiable at a glance. Retype the new drafts to copy. Do what journalists do to ensure identification: Put a date and a project title at the head of each separate sheet, along with a page number; type at the bottom 'Page 1 of 4' and so on; at the end of the copy type the word 'Ends' so that nobody goes looking for more; also sign it and show whether it is the first, second or final draft. Take a carbon or photocopy and keep it, or if you have a word processor, print out two copies. It is worth making a rubber stamp bearing your church's name and address with which to mark the reverse of each sheet, artwork, envelope – anything.

Doing the Reporting

Your Reporter will be mainly involved in offering stories or information to the local media, keeping local notice-boards 'fed', and developing relations with local business people and neighbourhood social groups. Most such work will happen in advance of your church's planned events or appeals as this gives a focus for all concerned. It is also true that every volunteer helper must have pauses from the pressure if she or he is to maintain enthusiasm.

At first, the two essential tasks will be to build up the contact list and to make sure that the information reaches the 'channels' in a suitable and instantly identifiable form, clearly issuing from your church. It would help to have a set of coloured stickers overprinted with your church nameplate and the Reporter's name and telephone number. By your use of envelopes of the same bright colour, all recipients will become familiar with materials coming from you, even before they read the contents. If those contents also prove to be useful to local journalists or broadcasters and others, then that familiarity will prompt them to use your offerings more and more readily.

You will need typed-up materials for most of these report-ings of your activities. The Reporter may ask the Writer to prepare these messages or may draft them for the Writer to edit and polish. It is vital that the Reporter co-ordinates his efforts with those of the group, so he must plan regular note-comparing sessions with the Chaser. The Leader should occasionally sit in on these to make sure that the Reporter's projection of the church and its key representatives is harmonious and true.

Guiding Principles

Accuracy of information is vital When working ahead of the group's events the Reporter must work closely with the Chaser to ensure that dates, times, names, venues, addresses and telephone numbers are current – and to correct any wrong information already sent out.

Understand the audience your channel serves Study the way the local newspaper, social group's newsletter or firm's notice-board works, how subjects are treated or displayed. Do the recipients like photographs? Do they prefer facts or human interest items? How much space does the channel routinely give to your kind of item? How long is the life of an item? Having understood the various mechanisms, offer only appropriate materials. A four-page press release that will be boiled down to two brief paragraphs in print not only dumps someone with an unnecessarily hard task of sub-editing, it may well guarantee the item is never read at all.

Supply pictures that make a point Pictures of people grinning at the camera, or posed in a frozen handshake at a presentation are the kind most editorial people can well live without. Whatever the point of your forthcoming project, use the picture to encapsulate it. If, say, you are organising a school event where the midday meal is to be replaced on one day by the typical rice diet of a Third world child, let the picture demonstrate the contrast by having a child sit before the two plates.

If you have a camera enthusiast in your group, talk him into restricting the pictures to black and white. Colour prints appear rather blurred in monochrome – which is the likely reproduction method of almost all your channels. Better still, if your enthusiast also has a small darkroom, let him use this to keep your costs down. Offer the media prints no smaller than 8″ x 6″ and preferably with a surface called 'unglazed glossy', which allows the layout team to retouch a picture or 'white-round' easily. Identify every print with your church name-plate, the media contact's name and address; then attach a label with an instructive caption. You might use a rubber stamp for the identity purpose – as advised to the Writer – and you will find packs of cheap self-adhesive labels in big stationery stores. For the caption labels, in addition to the story information given, also create a reference code which will help your photographer to trace the negative should further prints be needed.

If there is no photographer in the group, get to know the local newspaper's cameraman; by asking him sparingly and only when you have a worthwhile subject, you may not only get some at-cost pictures, but also an entree to his newspaper. Alternatively, put an invitation on the notice-board of the local tech inviting photographic enthusiasts to ring you; or ask the local secondary school head to suggest someone.

Always have something to offer Make your media outlets feel that a message from you is always positive. When it is time to reestablish a contact, try to offer something helpful, but if your own group has no news at the time, by all means share something another group is doing. By the very process of contacting various local channels, both commercial and private, the Reporter becomes a channel himself. If you can do a good turn by publicising the local college Rag Week, do so readily. This kind of reciprocation helps everyone.

Quote only quoteworthy words Editors like 'verbatims', but only when they are strong, informative, and of warm human interest. There really is little point in putting quotation marks round some dull statement of policy intention to pretend it was said conversationally. That is what newspapers call 'puff'.

Follow-up your submissions When sending feature articles or calendars of events, ring up to check they have been received, not to pester, just to be – and be seen to be – efficient.

Write letters Newspaper letter pages are free and not at all difficult to get into. Ask team members to submit letters on subjects related to your forthcoming events. With the help of the Writer keep them brief, lively, informative and challenging. Above all, keep them coming.

Prepare radio releases If you have a local radio station, start by listening to a full week's programmes to identify where news or features about local community life are scheduled. With a stop-watch, time the duration of all such items to find an average length. Then prepare your group's stories to those 'slots'. An unhurried voice can deliver 150 words in a minute, which means that if your best opportunity is fifteen seconds-worth at the end of a local news round-up, you have perhaps 35 words to express an idea as well as communicate essential facts. If what you were hoping to say can't be said this briefly, find a different subject. Having prepared the message with your Writer, have it typed, double-spaced, on an A5 sheet, used sideways. Put a heading over the story which will catch the producer's eye. Write the message to be read aloud, which means eliminating too many sibilants that hiss and splutter. Keep the sentences short and bright. Keep the style relaxed even if the subject is serious; newsreaders give only disasters the heavy news treatment.

Audition your group Discover the voices that record best, identifying the people who can respond to questioning in a lively way. If you have some good performers, set about getting them dates as local speakers, or interviews on local radio; get them to call in to listener phone-in programmes to

121

publicise your events. If you have any access at all to a regional TV station and one or more of your group might do well on that medium, consider enrolling him in a short TV-performers' course if your budget allows it; this teaches how to be comfortable in a studio and to handle questions well.

Send to these addresses for more information:

CTVC Hillside, Merry Hill Road, Bushey, Watford, Hertfordshire WD2 1DR. Tel: 01-950 4426.

Christian Broadcast Training Ltd Severals House, Bury Road, Newmarket, Suffolk, CB8 7BS. Tel: 0638 668491.

Say thank-you The best contact people are also the most busy and frayed. And like all pressurised people, they begin to feel dehumanised. They will be heartened when you deal graciously with them being direct and *not* wasting their time. In particular, following a recent contact, whether or not your offering was used, thank them for their attention. This can be a brief message left on their answering machine or a line on a postcard.

Doing the Designing

To repeat: you do not need to be an artist to be the group's Designer, but you need to be a practical, resourceful person with a good visual sense. As taste in things visual is highly subjective; the aim here must be to express your church's persona, not your own. Somewhere between the negatively impersonal or insipid and the wildly partisan or experimental, your way of solving problems will find its place. What follows in this section is a set of practical aids towards finding that place.

Graphic Design Principles

Put the needs of the message before personal inclination Demonstrations of your own skill, sense of humour or point of

122

view should not become a focus for attention. Such things are permissible only as ways of sharpening the reader's attention.

Let the nature of the message determine the style of design
Even professionals fall into the trap of bringing to any given message a preconceived idea, something they are expecting to build in. This invariably conflicts with the smooth transmission of an idea. If the subject is lighthearted – a celebration or a seasonal bazaar, perhaps – then a decorative or fanciful approach may be appropriate. If it carries an altogether different weight of message – say a challenge to mission or an appeal for support in a dramatic cause – then a strong, simple graphic presentation is essential. Let the message show you how to present it.

Do not let the words and the visual conflict Sometimes, where the text message is somewhat sombre (and be sure in that case that you really wish it to be!) a pointed visual idea can express the essence of the intention more potently. Where the text message is saying 'Bring and Buy Sale' the visual message can sharpen the transmission by showing examples of items on sale or by introducing a cartoon figure to humanise the appeal of the event. Where the word message carries its own immediacy and impact – such as 'SOS – Save Our Souls!' then the Designer need do no more than emphasise the meaning with dramatic lettering (which the professionals would regard as typographic design).

Use one message at a time At first, a Designer is grateful to hit upon any workable idea at all, but remember that once a skill begins to develop, so may an insidious desire to 'perform'. For any one message a Designer may find two, three or more suitable ideas. Choose and use just the one. More than one idea in one design – as in one text – only splits attention. Discard surplus ideas without flinching and trust absolutely that as you've found yourself rich in ideas once, so you will always be. The Lord will inspire as long as your unselfish concern is to let the message shine through.

Always plan a 'route' Every design, however complex, is

essentially a journey of understanding for a reader. In our culture we have learned to read from left to right, sequentially, phrase by phrase. From exposure to countless commercial messages we learn to decode headlines that compress fact or ideas. We absorb symbolic visual codes that stand instantly for entire ideas (a red hand conveys 'stop' in a way more chilling than the word itself). The famous 'I love New York' design by Milton Glaser: letter 'I', a heart shape, letters 'N' and 'Y', has been adapted cross-culturally everywhere from here to Tokyo and now reads instantly as a pattern, before the letters themselves can be read.

All these considerations must operate to a greater or lesser extent in all designs. Where should a reader start? What should strike him first? Which items serve to amplify understanding, and which indicate the reactions you wish? The reader wishes to grasp your message in a sequential, orderly fashion until the moment he loses interest, and the responsibility for his attention is yours – the Designer's. If you allow the reader to take in secondary information first, comprehension is ruptured; you are making the reader work too hard, and most will not bother. To accomplish a speedy, engaging journey through a message, you must order elements well – not in top-to-bottom order like a Victorian theatre bill or a tombstone, but in order of emphasis and related meaning, so that the eye hops from one stage to the next. This is called layout, the technique by which the thoughtful designer can become effective at once, if not polished in his skills. A headline can set the topic; an associated picture can dramatise and particularise its meaning; a subheading can introduce the next step desired, tempting the reader to consider the appeal of the text; a proposition ('tickets available only until Saturday') will encourage action; and a coupon will facilitate it. Plan the route. Do not allow lapses in attention. Create an arrival point, and guide the reader all the way.

Design to your audience In the early days of their newly-discovered technology, computer manufacturers addressed prospective buyers with a high-tech language of text and visuals. They knew their products were needed and that the market was

124

paying attention, but unfortunately they failed to communicate at the level of their readers' understanding, and as a consequence may have delayed the computer age by some years. Similarly, even at the level of your own church's reaching out, do not design anything until the nature of your audience is utterly clear. If your Writer's text doesn't reveal this kind of awareness, encourage a rewrite. If some pictorial element seems a good idea, think about the right image to arrest or inform your particular audience. The young will not take to nostalgic images, while the elderly will. Don't put the wrong pictures in just to 'brighten up' the material.

Go for less rather than more Just as the pauses between notes contribute vitally to a musical composition, so does white space in a layout. Correct use of space gives you more freedom to vary the scale of elements within the design area; quite complicated designs can thus be made to seem simple and unfussy. It is the density of text in a legal document that makes it so formidable, but well distributed white space makes the route from one item to the next quite clear. If you do not have the room, use more pages or cut the length of the text.

Vary your emphases Correct emphasis depends on the content and intention of the message and must be judged carefully. Intriguing variations in scale are your main tool of emphasis, not a hysterical and bewildering battery of underlinings, exclamation marks and sentences in capital letters. Small but intensely bold letters will catch the eye quicker than letters twice the size but of a light, spidery outline. An illustration taking up a big area but showing a full length figure will seem smaller than a half-size picture showing a close-up.

A simple test of scale is to look at the separate elements of your layout: a panel of text is one, a headline another, a drawing another, the church's name and symbol another – and so on. Half close your eyes and read these elements as comparative 'weights'. The text may cover a large area but is a light grey element and therefore 'weighs less'. By looking for weight, not measurable size, you can discover what scale exists. If all elements weigh the same, you have a scale-less design which does not draw the reader in and is dull. To improve matters, bearing in mind your intent, make your headline bigger or bolder, or the key image in the illustration smaller. Once a good contrast in scale is established – and note we say 'good' rather than 'right', as there are always several ways to achieve the same effect – the reader wants to continue to look and read. Start juggling with scale, and soon you develop your own standards and a smooth method that can make design layout seem easy.

Balance the design Having fixed your scale, you see that the elements are juxtaposed properly. An asymmetric layout – one where the balance, though there overall, does not obviously strike the eye – is often used. Typically, elements are spread wider to leave uneven dispositions of white space. If there is a large weight over to the left, high up, there will be another of similar weight low to the right – or perhaps two closely sited elements whose aggregate weight 'balances' the other. The asymmetric layout is like a body in motion; it has force and energy – which make it appropriate for newspaper design or posters enjoining us to act positively. When we want a slow, thoughtful reaction, however, or when we wish to give due weight to a serious proposition, a centred or almost centred layout works best.

Use colour sparingly Your group's finances will almost certainly find that lavish use of colour in printing is out of reach. Yet should the option be open to you, be parsimonious, and under-use it. This is a more difficult aspect of design for the non-professional. Home-made designs break up an area of bold lettering by stressing key words in red to contrast against the black, the result being the reverse of the intention as the red – being lighter in tone than the black – seems to recede in importance. To make that concept work, the red letters would also have to be typeset in a heavier weight – not an easy balance to strike.

When designing for white letters to show through a coloured ground, be sure that if you also want black lettering to overprint some areas of the colour, the colour is in its tone exactly between

126

white and black, otherwise a wrong emphasis will occur.

At the balancing stage, regard colour as just another element, using it to represent only one or two elements and never spotting it about all over the area. At first, then, use colour for contrast – a solid shape to carry white headline letters, a single decorative border, a rectangle behind an illustration – make it the focus of the reader's attention. Avoid the use of colour for detailed emphasis such as underlining headlines or odd words here and there.

If you are using a dark colour as a substitute for black, take care if there are to be photographic illustrations of people: they look fine in dark sepia (if a bit old-fashioned), but dreadful in purple, emerald green or viridian. Be particularly careful about fluorescent colour in display items. The optical disturbance which attracts attention in the first place can be too irritating for tender eyes to want to look further at the message. Never use two fluorescent colours together.

Colour may be used well as a colour coding – a regularly used signal that a particular message does indeed come from your church. This can work if you make many messages at frequent intervals. Colour alone will not achieve this instant recognition, but used in conjunction with key words and symbols it will eventually become familiar to your audiences. If you choose to do this, selecting perhaps a particular shade of blue, note that the absorbency characteristics of different paper surfaces and different printing methods will make that same blue appear inconsistent. Ask for a printer's advice.

As earlier mentioned, some groups will preprint elements of a regularly needed design element – the drawing of their church or a Christian symbol – in a colour, so that subsequent messages can be over-printed in black or a contrasting colour to give a more arresting effect. But keep such designs to the perimeters of the layout – along the top edge, in a corner, as a border or a baseline device, leaving a clean, uncluttered space for the later printing. Wrongly registered printing which overlaps looks so sloppy; you would have done better to stay with a single printing.

Don't be afraid to use 'swipes' Plagiarising other designers' solutions is not permissable, but do not shrink from adapting the thinking behind someone else's idea to your purpose. If you really think something is right for you, boldly ask if you may borrow the artwork; for non-commercial purposes, people will usually say yes. Your Forager can do this for you. Other churches may be tolerant about swiping, but commercial firms may well act against you. Do bear in mind that (commercial firms aside) the copyright of an illustration or cartoon belongs to its originator and the use of it without permission is stealing. By all means swipe freely from decorative elements or illustrations from books out of copyright; there are books of old art assembled from such sources, published expressly as design resources. Most will have a quaint, period quality, though they may suit some designs. The only exception to the 'do not swipe, ask' rule is in the matter of collages. If you take minor elements from a number of different published design elements and make up a composite illustration, nobody is going to sue or even complain. This is the graphic equivalent of the theatrical management's use of critics' quotations and is a process within the capability of most new designers; check with the Fixer first, though, that the print process to be used will not reduce the collage to a blotchy confusion; if in doubt use only 'line' illustrations or decoration (those without graduated grey-tones or colours).

Central libraries may carry reference books of printed ephemera gathered from nineteenth century sources. Collections of early art in advertisements, music sheets or children's books from Britain and the Continent will often offer borders, cartouches, decorative elements and other adaptable details. Big libraries will usually make photocopies for a few pence of the pages you want. Better still, haunt the second-hand bookshops for your own 'swipe' sources.

Get your geometry right A novice Designer has every excuse for being tentative about the layout but none at all for assembling the artwork all askew. The first task takes experience, the second mainly careful attention. The outside area of the layout measured correctly and its right angles each measure 90°. Inside that area, upright columns of text should be parallel, and headlines should not sink to one side. See under *Artwork Preparation*, pages 146-148.

Keep your artwork safe Prepare it cleanly, placing a paper flap across the design surface to keep it from inky fingers and coffee mugs. If possible make a simple cardboard sleeve for it, the description and date clearly marked for later retrieval. You may want to reprint it later, or peel up elements to be used again on new artwork. It should be stored flat and away from extremes of temperature or humidity. Your Fixer may wish to file these pieces along with printing plates and have a periodical review of what is, or is not worth keeping. Tell your Fixer routinely to see that the artwork is returned from printers, who have a nasty habit of mislaying it.

Enjoy the process If your group's programme is too taxing ask for help. Designs go wrong if you feel resentful.

Read the principles addressed to the Writer See pages 109-118.

Equipment

This suggested list for preliminary design equipment assumes the Designer will be producing artwork mainly for one-colour printing. The items should be purchased from a graphic design suppliers rather than from a fine art materials shop.

    ★ One 18″ steel rule calibrated for inches on one side, centimetres on the other. It will be useful for ruling lines, for measuring and as a cutting edge which will not be made uneven by sharp blades.

    ★ One clear plastic set square measuring 12″ along the tall right angle side. A smaller size makes marking out areas of A4 tedious.

    ★ One metal scalpel and set of steel blades, essential for precise paper cutting.

    ★ One tin of Cow Gum, the petroleum jelly adhesive ideal for sticking down pieces of paper onto other pieces of paper without wrinkling. When smeared thinly on both contact surfaces with the aid of a plastic spreader or finger it has the great virtues of not drying instantly and so allowing positional adjustment, it allows later peeling-up with the aid of petrol lighter fluid (its solvent); Also gum smears can be magically cleaned up, with no trace on the surface, with the aid of an eraser made up of Cow Gum rubbed from the edges of artwork which builds up into a knobbly lump. The vapour is strong and flammable but even so essential.

★ Putty erasers, ideal for pencil marks. Do not use hard erasers.

★ One Rapidograph and, if you can afford it, a set of insertable 'nibs'. These drawing pens have a reservoir to take black drawing ink and will produce an absolutely even line of set thickness and flow. The insert points will range from a delicate hairline to a thick one useful for heavy underlining. Use this instrument for the keylines for artwork (the indications to the printer of where the page is to be trimmed), and for any straight-line drawing such as column break-lines, borders around pictures and, if you must, stencil letter drawing.

★ One container of Rapidograph ink.

★ One container of typist's correction fluid, to smarten up ink smears, lines that stray over the edge; it has the advantage of not showing up at the platemakers' negative stage and so not allowing all those strange smears often seen on cheap printing.

★ One roll of half-inch magic tape, which is not the usual transparent sticky tape, but a low-tack version on which you can draw in ink. Also useful for attaching paper overlays.

★ One A2 pad of smooth cartridge paper, on the sheets of which most of your artwork can be Cow-gummed. Used horizontally it is large enough to allow two A4 areas side by side and borders all round. The cardboard backs of these pads can be made into carry-sleeves for art-work. Do not, by the way, allow a ballpoint pen anywhere near your artwork as the pressure of a point can track through several layers of cartridge to leave a booby-trap channel for later Rapidograph lines; nor should you ever write on the reverse of a photoprint as the indent of a ballpoint will reproduce as a line when printed.

★ One A3 pad of typographer's detail paper. This translucent paper is not as thick as tracing paper yet almost as transparent and useful for tracings, layouts and overlay sheets for finished artwork, allowing you to view without having constantly to bare the artwork surface.

★ Other items such as dry transfer lettering can be bought as needed.

★ To complete the Designer's equipment, you'll need a wide table and an angle-poise lamp. A drawing board with a T-square would be a luxury, but unnecessary unless your ambitions grow. Similarly, a plastic cutting board – a wonderful surface that seems to resist any scoring from scalpels – can be substituted by the cardboard backs of layout pads. Some reference materials will be helpful and will soon accumulate as the Fixer brings you printers' typesheets and other aids to specifying; paper makers will send samples of coloured papers; and a visit to a major printing exhibition will stock you with all kinds of free aids and references.

Printing/Reproduction Methods

Though this is not really the Designer's main concern, you will need to understand how the reproduction process affects the way your artwork is prepared. Ideally, you should join with the Fixer in a fact-finding mission in your area, scouting out the economical printers and the service they offer. If you ask, printers will give you a demonstration. Your new knowledge will stop all sorts of minor mistakes and waste of money.

What follows is a broad listing of the kinds of printing you might encounter, along with an indication of which kinds of print-work go with which process.

Stencil Machines There are relatively sophisticated new

versions of this process, but since you probably won't be using one unless someone has donated his old office version, let us say that they are useful for one colour only printing of a very basic type. 'Artwork' for them is usually of the typed stencil kind where the typewriter key bites its imprint into a surface which will eventually deliver an ink version. It is sometimes possible to add decorative elements and even bold headlines using a stylus to scratch an image onto the stencil. More up-to-date systems will allow any kind of drawn 'line' image to be reproduced. A characteristic of the images produced is that at the end of the run everything gets greyer and greyer, or blotchier. Coupled with an elderly portable typewriter whose keys are worn and unaligned, stencil copiers have produced some of the least legible printing known to civilisation, but they are of course cheap to run.

'Instant Print' Shops are able to produce reasonably neat images from flat artwork at a bearable cost. They can print in thousands, using a paper plate (which wears out to make poor images at the end of a longish run), or synthetic plates which are of higher quality. They can print on many different papers, on light card, and in simple two colour. It is impossible to define the limits of the service, partly because the machines keep being improved and partly because some such printers also offer conventional printing presses at a higher price. As a general rule, use these shops only for designs when you are printing black images on white paper and when you do not require evenly printed large areas of solid colour. Such establishments will not as a rule offer typesetting, though some do; others will have a design service attached to the print shop.

Office photocopiers The plain paper type are useful. (Those which can use only the slimy-surfaced special photosensitive paper are not worth considering as they are limiting.) Some of these machines deliver good quality photographic repro-duction as well as 'line' images. They allow the flexibility of copying onto coloured paper or white stock of sizes from A4 or A3 – some up to A2. The image will be black and the unit cost (price per sheet after paper, printing medium and hire cost is calculated) is prohibitive for long runs. If you want small, controllable runs and you own a machine, it will serve you well. Your Forager might set about convincing a local business to donate one that is being replaced.

Letterpress was the prime printing method until 20 years ago. Such printers usually offer typesetting services; and because the letters are individually assembled, corrections are fairly simple up to the very last moment before printing. This makes the method useful for urgent, topical work, but on the whole expensive for most of your needs. Unless you are fortunate enough to have one of the 'master printer' services locally, reserve this method for smart, special commemorative items such as invitation cards on high quality papers.

Lithographic Printing is the principle method available and capable of handling print runs from as few as a hundred up to long runs of thousands. The better litho printers can offer high fidelity reproduction in almost any combination of paper, colour or shape, including full-colour reproduction. Your Fixer must shop around to find the best combination of quality and price.

Silkscreen Printing is an old method made modern by latest machinery. The crafts section of your local library will probably carry reference books on this subject. One written for schools' use may be of most help, but if there are none ask them to order *Silk Screen Techniques* by Biegeleisen and Cohn, Dover Publications of New York. A print shop locally may still cut the screen stencils by hand, though now it is done photographically. The advantage of this method for your group is that it is ideal for quite small runs of high quality images. As its ink is thicker, silkscreen is mostly used for display purposes. It can print on fabric, plastic, wood – anything that can be stretched into a flat surface. The principle is so simple that your group could even make its own screen-print room.

Some printers offer a design service, but you must be clear about what is on offer. A trained designer and a studio artwork service, will be expensive, though professional-looking. If the printer offers to 'lay it out' himself, you are getting an untrained designer giving you the benefit of his practical experience, which may or may not be worth having; only you can judge. If the print job is sufficiently rewarding, this layout may be done free. Should such an offer be made, leave an approximate layout (or an exact one as you become more able) for him to follow and adapt. Working in this way with the right sort of local printer can produce acceptable work and is the only real alternative to making the artwork yourself.

Images may be reproduced in a variety of ways other than by reprographics and the traditional methods, but most carry an unacceptably high price tag. Do not hesitate to encourage your Fixer to collect price comparisons for everything from photoprinting to slidemaking, from videotaping to computer printouts.

On pp 134-139 below, guidance will be given in the assembly of simple artwork for printing reproduction.

Visual Images

The simplest kind of image you can make is one drawn in black ink. This is called 'line' and as long as the sketch, diagram or cartoon is rendered on white paper in a dense black, the printer's camera can turn it into a plate without reducing the quality. The illustration can be quite delicate (fine line), but take care not to draw it so fine that when you have it reduced, the white space 'fills in'.

As a general rule, draw all your artwork to the actual size you want it to appear when printed. Enlargement and reduction are possible, but once you wish to have variations within the same printing, costs zoom up and errors multiply.

If you find that preparing artwork to the same size as the intended printed area is too fiddly, work to 'half-up'. This means making both the length and width half as long again. The simple technique of scaling will be explained further on, pp 137-138.

After line illustrations come 'full tone' images, such as photographs or simple drawings using washes of one-colour tones in indian ink or water colour. When using white paint to correct such originals, take care to use Process White, which reproduces cleanly. It is likely that most of your printing will be done by a photo/litho process where the cost of including tone illustrations is relatively inexpensive. Should you be using letterpress printers, a separate block has to be made and can prove prohibitive. At first, your Designer will be well advised to find photos or illustrations which are the right size to stick directly onto the artwork, either the same size or half-up; a photo/litho printer can then make a single plate from it with the minimum of preparation. Later, cost permitting, you can supply the printer with various elements, all scaled correctly for him to assemble into a single plate.

Should you wish to use colour there are two basic types of artwork to understand. The simpler is where you intend to use 'colour line' – i.e. one or more printings in addition to your base colour (usually black), to be printed in register, say, black plus red, or black plus blue plus red. For each printing a new plate must be made from a separate original – usually prepared by putting the printing you intend to be black on the artwork and overlaying the artwork with sheets of art-film, one overlay for each additional colour; these extra colour originals are also drawn in black with black type or lettering as the printer's camera finds this simplest. To ensure that the ultimate registration of printed colour is perfect, it is essential to trace through onto each overlay the keymarks drawn on the base artwork (black printing), so that the printer can reproduce each element to exactly the same scale. The keymarks indicate the final trimmed area of paper and folding positions if needed. See artwork preparation on p 146.

Four-colour process – the term used to describe reproduction of images in full colour, as in colour photos or full-colour drawings using continuous tonal effects – is extremely expensive and will rarely fit your budget. Should you wish to produce a glossy brochure or a four-colour poster, this will involve the printer in a colour separation process designed to simulate full colour through the use of black, yellow, cyan (blue) and magenta. When that time comes, talk to your printer about artwork preparation.

Two easily understood skills essential to the Designer are 'masking' and 'scaling'. These have to do with the selection and preparation of images for reproduction.

Masking This elementary but transforming method gets the best effect from any given illustration, especially photographs. Its purpose is to deliver to the chosen audience the area of the image that will best suit the mood and purpose of your message. Suppose you have a photo of a man walking across an open area showing much landscape and sky all round. If your purpose was to demonstrate the value of open-air exercise you would probably choose to leave in most of the picture; if the identity of the person was critical to the message you would 'close-in' on the figure, showing perhaps his head and shoulders and down to his waist; if you wanted to dramatise a text discussing a person's state of mind, you might crop the photo even closer, probably to include the head or facial features only; if your layout demanded a tall shape from a photo that was wide, you might crop the figure down the line of his back so that even in the narrow space he is 'walking-into' the picture. You may also cut out the image from the background by a careful 'whiting-out' around the figure with process white paint; this is only worth attempting when the shape desired has a clean, unfussy outline and where the background consists of plain, uncluttered tones. Never use this white paint round a person's face unless the photo image is large – nothing looks worse than a frayed human profile!

Masking can alter impact, focus and effect. An excellent book on this and other related techniques is Harold Evans' *Pictures on a Page,* published by Heinemann; it is available in libraries and is one of a set on newspaper production. As you may not have access to the type of viewing camera which professional designers use, here is a simple version requiring only a sheet of black card.

Make two 'L' shaped cut-outs using a scalpel and metal edge, not scissors. These may be of a size to suit you, but something measuring 12″ at its shortside, 18″ at its long side and 2″ wide will serve most masking purposes. By laying one 'L' the right way up and the other upside down, you can create a central space which can be altered to any right-angled shape, square, wide or tall. Placed over a photo it allows you to discover the ideal cropping and shape. This framing, or masking of the photo can be used to match the actual space you have allowed in your layout for the picture area; here you simply frame the desired area with the two 'L' shapes, perhaps fixing them with a spot of blue-tack before laying over the photo to discover the ideal position; when you have so decided, slip a sheet of detail paper between the mask and the photo, carefully keeping the position, then trace with a fibre-tip pen (not a ballpoint) the main elements of the photo-image, also marking a dot in each corner to indicate the masked area; after taping the detail paper to the top edge of the photoprint join up the dots, checking that the area outlined is geometrically correct with the aid of a ruler and set square. This is then a guide to the printer in making his plate or, if the print is not precious for some other use, a guide for you to slice through the detail and photo paper and make a neat, accurate cut-out shape to be stuck directly onto your artwork. Where the size of the photo is much larger or smaller than the artwork you are assembling, you will need to *scale* the photo so that the printer can enlarge or reduce it to fit the precise area you have left on the base artwork.

Scaling is the sister skill to masking. Given that you have decided on the space put aside on the layout or artwork for

Scaling   **Masking**

the photo, and that the actual photo is either too small or too large, you need to indicate an area on the photo which will enlarge or reduce in perfect proportion to fit it. This is an elementary technique. First trace off accurately on detail paper the *exact* shape available on the layout; position this traced image (which must be geometrically square) towards the bottom left-hand corner of the artwork sheet and then draw a diagonal from the bottom left corner of the traced area through the top right corner – and on as far as there is room. Take one of your masking 'Ls' and blue-tack it over the detail paper to match the left-hand and base lines of the traced area; lay this over the photo and bring the other inverted 'L' in position so that its junction point touches the diagonal line you've drawn; by sliding this 'L' up and down the diagonal in conjunction with the other 'L' you can decide on the best place to mask the photo. As described under *masking* above, trace the image features on the detail paper, pinpoint the corners of the area, draw in the area, fix the overlay to the photo and then, finally, mark in red felt-tip the instruction to the printer – either 'enlarge/reduce area marked to X''', giving either the depth *or* the width of the area marked on your layout. The printer will then photographically scale the photo to fit.

These two basic skills will make your work look better and eliminate unnecessary correction costs. (As an exercise, look through an old magazine and, using your masking 'Ls', see if you can improve the cropping of the pictures there; think of

138

variations in mood that might be demanded by the text and mask the pictures to get the best effect.) Note that drawings with ungeometric boundaries can nevertheless be masked and scaled in the same way. Simply 'contain' the drawing with a square or rectangle that touches its widest and deepest points, draw a diagonal as already described, and the procedure is the same as for photographs. The only design consideration here is that although it fits a notional rectangle, being uneven in outline, there will perhaps be a bias in visual 'weight' – a hole of white space, perhaps, or a concentration of black image close to one side – either of which may make you move the entire shape to a more visually satisfying position on the layout/artwork.

Text Preparation

If you were to calculate across a year's output of messages by your church you would find that at least 60% of the areas would be covered in text, rather than headlines or illustrations/symbols. It follows that words must be a primary part of a Designer's responsibility, to be treated for their meaning just as much for the space they must occupy. Leaving aside the text used in headlines (see pp 142-146 below), here we can consider text presentation, or *typography,* as it is known. In your artwork you have, for all practical purposes, three options: handwriting, typesetting or type-writing.

Handwriting To be used sparingly in printed materials, as it becomes tiring to read in quantity and often wasteful of space. For certain special effects, such as conveying a highly personal message or when you have the services of a skilled calligrapher, it can be effective. Although a short-cut and cost-saver, however, it can block reading.

Typesetting This term describes the translation of written text into mechanically or photographically generated letterforms. There are many typefaces from which to choose, though any printer you employ will work from a limited range offering a selection of faces, sizes and related variations. (Type-faces are often designed as families, giving a range of stresses based on the same characteristics from light to heavy, from upright to italic.) As a general rule, *serif* types – the more decorative letters – are easier to read when set in large areas, and *sans serif* types – block letters – give more impact when used in limited amounts. A safe rule for beginners is to stay within families of type, getting variations in effect by mixing weights and sizes. Until you gain confidence, limit any message to a maximum of two different families of type; use more and you'll bewilder the reader. The typesetter can change the effect of a column of type by increasing or reducing the amount of space left between the lines; more space makes an airier effect, less space a darker effect. Where photosetting is involved, this light/dark effect can be achieved also by letterspacing – by cramming the letters tighter or putting more 'air' between them. When using a letterpress printer who will assemble metal letters, the standard letterspacing will be sufficient for most uses. Such textural variations are for you to discuss with the printer and will be dependent on how many words must fit into a given space.

A simple test for how a section of text might fit an area on a layout is to draw up the area on detail paper, place it over an example of the typeface set in an alphabet line (printers will supply these on request), and count how many of the typeset characters will fit the width of your design area. You will have a number, say 60 characters. Then, including each space between words as one character, count sixty characters across the typewritten text the Writer has supplied and draw a vertical pencil line down the page at that point. All the lines to the left of the pencil border count as one printed line in the selected typeface, and the fragments of typewriting on the right of the pencil line can be roughly assessed in terms of full lines. So you might have 20 + 6 lines. If the printer has also supplied specimens of that typeface set in panels, it is a quick calculation to find how deep 26 of those lines will come. If this falls well short of the space allowed in your layout, consider going to the same typeface in a larger size; if it overruns, go down a size. If the disparity is much greater, get the Writer to cut or increase the text accordingly. Do not try to cram too many words into the space by going to the small type-sizes used on the back of insurance documents, or to inappropriately large sizes.

A panel of text may be set in 'fully justified' form – lined-up on its left and its right margins, or 'unjustified' – lined-up on its left only, with the right side left ragged. 'Centred' settings leave an uneven margin on both sides. Lining columns of type on the right, leaving the left unjustified is a device you should limit to captions for pictures, as the type looks chaotic in any quantity.

A *type mark-up* is the term for a complete instruction to a printer for fitting the type to the layout. This is a demanding skill gained only by experience and more instruction than can be given here, so your Designer should talk through the settings with the printer; she will learn by trial and error which treatments are most pleasing – another reason for limiting the range of type-families used. As a form of self-defence the Designer might collect samples of settings done by the printer for his other clients; from these she can select those which best suit your church's sort of message-making and, knowing the printer can offer those precise effects, base her type selections on them. From these working examples it will eventually be possible for the Designer to offer the Writer word-counts for panels of text *before* they are written.

Typewriting To make messages on a shoestring – at really low cost – there is much to be said for *not* relying on printer-set type unless the demands of the situation justify the extra expense. Someone in your group may be able to offer the use of a golf-ball or daisy-wheel kind of interchangable typeface typewriter. A fixed-face typewriter will do, though it will offer no variation in type 'texture' and, if it does not provide a carbon-ribbon's crisp, black imprint, will reproduce far less well. Portable machines using ink-coated material ribbons will always provide a blotchy, home-made look. If you are stuck with one, set your Forager to work among the business community; they're all busy moving from heavy electronic typewriters to computers and get very poor trade-in deals on their old machines, so ask and you may well receive.

With access to a type-change machine using interchangeable typefont systems such as daisywheels and golfballs, as well as a typist able to sit down with the Designer to produce printable text, almost any message can be made to look polished. The typist, by the way, has to be extremely patient as she may have to type several versions of a paragraph to get it fitting right without word-breaks too often at the ends of lines and other such unacceptables. As a minimum kit of spare golfball or daisywheel faces you should have one compact block-letter style such as *Gothic*, one more elegant serif-style such as *Bookface* – these to provide variation in columns of typing – and one extra-large letter style such as *Orator*, so useful for introductory paragraphs, crossheadings and similar emphases. In section on page 143 below, this typing technique is more fully explained.

Display Headlines

With the recent explosion of photosetting and computer programming, the designers of typefaces have been busy as never before. Scores of new, often eccentric letterforms have been born; traditional ones have been modernised or distorted photographically to give new effects. This pursuit of novelty has spoiled designers for choice and threatens to undo the amateur; the temptation to fill designs with quirky decorative typefaces has overwhelmed many a church message with every news item carrying its own typographical folly above – the overall effect bizarre or cluttered. For the essence of good design is control – and control means restraint. Like children making themselves ill in a chocolate factory, local political groups, social and charity organisations discover that they can give their messages a certain slickness so they burst into instant lettering with the sort of greed that leads to indigestion.

142

But there can be a more sensible approach. By all means buy a copy of Letraset's latest catalogue of designer-aids, including 150 or so rub-down 'instant lettering' typefaces in many sizes. But pass the selection through a few mental filters, avoiding those which are actually difficult to read, those which are frankly gimmicky – they quickly become boring and will date your messages – those which, when used for more than two or three words, become too exotic, those not offering a true family of weights – thus inhibiting your ability to vary emphasis – above all avoiding those which do not look like an expression of your church's work. From the survivors, look for two – at the most three – families which might form your typographical palette. One should be a bold blockletter family such as Gill, Franklin Gothic, Antique Olive, Folio, Futura, Helvetica or Univers. One should be a 'classic' serif face such as Caslon, Century, Palatino, Plantin, Souvenir or Times. A third, if you must, could be one of the functional families such as Beton/Rockwell, Optima, American Typewriter, Italia or Lubalin Graph. Remember, in a newsheet when using only one typeface, you have the variations available of upper and lower case (capital and small letters); add one more size of the same face and you have four variations; add two more weights in two sizes from the same type family and you have eight variables. A useful motto here is, be liberal in your design thinking, be conservative in the implementation.

Making up a Headline This is simple to do and only a little harder to do outstandingly well. The dry transfer sheet is arranged so that each letter has below it at an absolutely consistent level, a marker line; this, when you align it with a pencilled line drawn on your artwork, will guarantee that the letters transferred will be neatly in a line. To do this right takes only a little practice. Where you buy your lettering sheets you will be able to get a plastic spatula designed to rub down the letters. Obey the keeping conditions suggested by the manufacturer. Having rubbed down a full line of letters, place the

143

waxed protective sheet provided over the line and use the spatula to burnish flat the lettering. Should you rub down a letter all askew or in some way damage a letter during transfer, use your home-made Cow Gum eraser (see p 130) to take the offending character away.

To get all the lines of your transferred letters absolutely level, begin by drawing a left-hand side pencil vertical and by laying your set-square's right-angle against it make a square horizontal line on which to align the instant letters. For second and subsequent lines, always run off this vertical. If you are rubbing letters directly onto finished artwork, use the left side trim marks as your guide. If you are making headlines on separate sheets, meaning to gum them to the main artwork later, start with a fresh pencil vertical. Having completed a full line, make a pencil dot for the alignment of the headline to follow, draw a true pencil horizontal through it, then erase the top pencil line before continuing on the second line. The lettering catalogue will give diagrams of these points, and your Designer will rapidly become adept at the physical process.

The *spacing* skill takes a little longer. Practice on the spacing between lines: too little allowed and the ascenders of the lower line – the b, d, f, h, k, l and t – and all the capital letters, will clash with the descenders of the top line – the g, j, p, q and y – and will tangle like a thicket; too much and the lines seem to float apart. To make a headline running into two or more lines look compact, a small overlap between the descender and ascender lines is desirable, but always – *before* embarking on the lettering – do a rough tracing on detail paper to establish if any such tangles are likely. (A rough length-of-line estimate is worth doing for general layout purposes, as where a phrase is broken makes a lot of difference to its impact.) Again, if a clash between ascenders and descenders seems imminent, try shifting the whole of the second line a little to the left or right – and if there's a third line to come, shift the position of that in the opposite direction, ending with three lines all 'staggered' but achieving an overall asymmetric balance.

144

Calling all rattlers: get collecting for the Famine in Ethiopia

Calling all rattlers: get collecting for the Famine in Ethiopia

To make instant headlines work best, concentrate above all on letterspacing. The simple principle here is to achieve an evenness of texture throughout a line of words. You may choose to crush up your letters to make a strong, dark, urgent effect, or open them out to give a considered, slower, more dignified effect – either way it is the even flow that matters. Working against you in this is that the geometry of the letters can be most unaccommodating in some typefaces. Certain combinations of letters will create either bunching of upright shapes or spreading of undesirable white spaces. Type left like that will strain the reader's comprehension, albeit unconsciously. Our brains do a lot of guess-reading, and if the basic building-blocks of the letters are awkwardly positioned, the flow of understanding will be impeded. If the letterspacing allows seeming gaps in the middle of a word or seems to bring two separate words together, a subtle confusion must follow. Take for example the phrase:

One million will be there

Note how the verticals create a compression and that between the end of one word and the start of the next, the standard word space is insufficient to let the break read. This is better:

One million will be there

Putting extra spacing between verticals and opening up word spaces will demand more space but will aid comprehension. Capital letters create their own kind of problem.

LONG-AWAITED EVENT

Here there are pockets of unhelpful space between some let-ters and compressions between others. More space between the AWA and the EN sections and the flow is much improved:

LONG-AWAITED EVENT

All you need do is distribute the *space* between letters so that each occupies roughly the same area. Think it through first, and if bad gaps or compressions are likely, adjust the spacing from the first letter on.

When using dry transfer letters, unless you are using an artboard surface, slip a sheet of flat card below the receiving surface. This will make the transfer smooth and will stop any bumps or gaps of the table's surface from breaking up the fragile letters.

Artwork Preparation

To recapitulate: If your church's finances allow, your Designer may be able to produce some printed work using typesetting, perhaps using the printer's own studio to prepare the artwork. This would save on effort if not on cash. For most churches this is rarely an option, and even where more budget is available messages will still have to be home-made. Tasks such as photographic displays, small numbers of notice-board posters, one-off banners for outdoor events – these things cannot always be passed to the professionals. The Designer will soon develop techniques for dealing with such eventualities, as practical sense is generally more helpful than a fertile imagination. Before we give information on the production of artwork for printed reproduction, though, here are a few general tips to help with artwork preparation.

Banners: For long-lived outdoor displays, buy PVC material sheeting of the kind children's raincoats are made of and paint the lettering with acrylic artist's paints; the acrylic, having some elasticity, will survive storage well. If you want to re-letter the banners later, silk-screen onto the PVC; methylated spirits will wipe clean the image.

Stand-up Displays For table-top displays not meant to be permanent, try the corrugated paper used for packing. With its ribbing placed vertically you can unwind a roll of the stuff, deciding on what kind of curving or concertina shape you'd like along the display area. Having plotted its path, surfaces intended to be flat need only a sheet of cardboard stapled to the side not facing the public. Along its length at intervals staple tall uprights of stiff cardboard, always at corners and cut slightly deeper than the corrugated paper. The base of these upright supports can be scored and turned under, later to be double-sided taped to the flat benchtop to create a footing. Some improvisation will be needed to keep everything secure. Two taut wires running at its top edge and fixed to walls at each end (like washing lines) will allow you to 'peg' the construction at various points. The non-corrugated front-facing surface can be painted, and paper items can be held in position with dressmaking pins by running the pins down and into the corrugated ribs.

Indoor Display Streamers For horizontal displays along walls or across stage curtains, for long, hanging pennants for the canopies of stalls and a dozen other uses, try wallpaper lining paper. It comes in rolls, is tough and cheap, and can be painted on with the kind of water-based powder colours used in primary schools – except be sure to mix them thickly to avoid running or undue crimping of the paper. How to paint bold, reasonably smart lettering? Draw four horizontal pencil lines along the length of lining paper, having unrolled it on a broad expanse like a stage or a long hallway; mark it out by first cutting a short strip to the depth of the lining paper, marking it off in sixths; at 18" intervals these divisions are marked along the length of paper and horizontal pencil lines are connected, leaving out the middle mark; the top and base line coincide with the paper's edges, which means four actual

147

lines are drawn in; the top of these makes a limit for the tops of capital letters and ascenders, the broader middle space is for the lower case letters and the lower line is the limit for descenders. The grid should look like this:

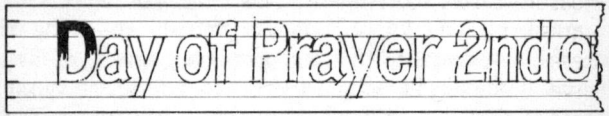

Roughly pencil double-line letters as above before filling in with colour. These strips can be rolled around the outside of postal tubes for safe storage should the message be usable another time. Be sure to put a strip of corrugated paper around each tube and to mark clearly on the outside what the message on the inside says.

Artwork on a Shoestring

The kind of printing you will be most likely to need will demand artwork prepared as flat copy, that is to say stuck down on one surface either to the same size as the intended printed piece, or half-up. The following suggestion is for a safe, simple, minimal method from which your Designer, once she gains confidence, can develop a style suitable to her own abilities and the group's needs. The format used here is that of an A4 newsletter, to be printed both sides in black. Here is a step-by-step description:

Define the Area A4 is a standard paper size measuring 297mm × 210mm (see also p 154 below). You have the artwork for two sides to assemble, but these can be laid side by side on the same artwork sheet. Take a sheet of A2 cartridge paper which, when used as a wide shape, will allow the two A4 areas to be marked in and still leave generous borders all round. The printer will make his negative from this, making separate plates, one for each side. Use paper masking tape to secure this sheet of cartridge to an absolutely smooth surface. Lay your 18″ rule parallel to the bottom edge and draw a baseline in pencil. Leaving wide margins right and left, tick off two 210mm measures along that baseline, leaving a 2.5cm gap between the two. Laying the rule back along this baseline and using the right angled upright of the set-square, draw four pencil vertical lines upwards from the tick marks. Measure an exact 297mm up each of the lines, then join these marks to form the top horizontal edge of the areas. Extend all these lines beyond the corners of the page areas and they will serve as keymarks. When the artwork is fully assembled, erase all other pencil lines, leaving only these inked-in marks for the printer to scale his plates and position the final printed image exactly within the areas.

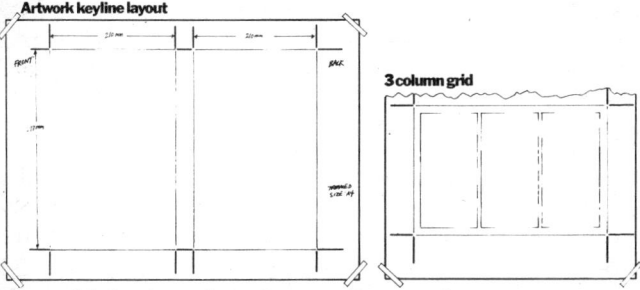

To establish where the columns of type and margins are to go, now draw in a pencil grid, the same layout for the front and back sides. Your first decision is, do you want one wide column, a two-column, or a three-column arrangement? A single column is too wide for anything save a very large display. A three-column grid makes columns far too narrow for typewritten text. A two-column grid allows some layout variety and an opportunity to use the larger typewriter faces (12 pica and Orator) to good effect. The layout shown here will use two equal-width columns, though you could make one wider than the other. If you really prefer a three-column grid, use the A4 area on its side. You must next decide whether you want the pages to have white borders all round, or whether you'd like some of the picture areas to 'bleed-off'. (A 'bleed' is where a photo image runs to the trimmed edge, and if you are using this kind of layout you must allow the picture to overlap the edges by 5mm so that if the printer is fractionally inaccurate with the paper-trimming after printing, there won't be a sliver of white edge showing where it shouldn't. This effect makes the page look more dramatic, and we'll use it in this demonstration.) Whether you bleed, or not, decide on a margin of at least 1cm. This grid uses 1.5cm borders all round, with a 1cm margin between the two columns; draw in the grid. No text or headline will overrun the borders, though headlines may straddle one or both columns.

Assemble the Text Gather everything that needs to go in. Do not start without every piece before you. Working as closely as possible with the Writer, decide on all the main headline messages and write them on a single sheet, indicating which are the lead headlines for each page before putting the remaining headlines into order of importance. Now type all the text, using your golfball or daisywheel typefaces. The idea is to produce what publishers call 'galleys': all the text produced to a standard column width, ready to be cut up and fitted to the layout grid. This is simple to do with a typewriter. Take a sheet of typing bond paper, which is light enough to allow 'show-through' and, laying it over the pencil grid on the artwork, trace off a column width. Using a black felt-tip pen, make this grid darker on the sheet. Now make a paper sandwich: with the black column grid facing you, place one sheet of the paper behind it and another in front of it. When you feed the sandwich into the typewriter the grid should show clearly through the top sheet and act as a guide to typing within the lines. The typist then aligns her left margin with the left vertical and types the text across up to, but not over, the right vertical. You must avoid too many word-breaks, as a right-hand edge bristling with dashes does not look too inviting. Judicious use of slightly longer or shorter paragraph indents and the occasional substituted word (in discussion with the Writer) can fill most lines comfortably. You must have clean type; retype a section rather than typing in minor corrections, which look scruffy when the work is printed. As you will eventually be cutting these galleys to gum down on the artwork, don't worry about retyping a section; simply cross out the rejected section. If the typewriter has 'pitch control', set it to the pitch which keeps the letters tightly together because it makes the typing look less airy, more like typesetting. For your main item or lead paragraph, you may choose to run across two columns using the Orator face (or equivalent), rather as national papers do with lead stories.

Once all the text is galleyed, but the headlines not yet prepared, a first, rough disposition of the elements between the front and back pages can be attempted. In doing this, allow spaces where the headlines might fit, checking your headline list for which has priority and which are long or short. A long, but less important headline can easily be set in one size too big and end up dominating the page, just as a short but important line can be undersized and fade from notice. As you do this mix-and-match exercise, look to weave the elements together, crossing the grid with headlines or illustration elements so that you don't end up with two ponderous stacks of words on each page. It will also become clear whether or not the illustrations can be fitted in comfortably, if they need to be changed or masked to a quite different shape. At this stage, the Writer and Designer, still working together, can assess whether there is a shortage or a surfeit of text and adjust accordingly. In general, a shortage of text is the easier problem as headlines or illustrations can be made larger to fill the gaps.

The nature of both message and audience must determine the balance of the message's elements: some demanding bold, dramatised effects with a large pictorial component, others needing a quieter, more informational style. Having made a rough disposition of elements it is time to make up your dry transfer headlines. With the transfer sheets before you – limited as suggested previously to two type families – and starting with the main headlines, rough-trace on detail paper the likely lengths of lines, trying to maintain the sense of a phrase when breaking up the lines. At this trace stage it will become apparent that some long lines need shortening, even that a longer adjective would make a better length; the Writer has the chance to exercise a creative spirit while maintaining the integrity of the editorial purpose.

Cut out the headlines with a scalpel, trimming them parallel with the text and within 5mm all round. When you come to gumming down the headline strips the 'squareness' of the cut will help you position neatly – a good reason for not trimming out with scissors. At this stage you still have time to rejuggle the elements, retype paragraphs, re-letter a headline, but once all the elements seem about right the paste-up may begin. Do one complete page at a time. Start by laying a clean A4 sheet over the artwork's A4 area and place without gumming each of the elements in its approximate position until you are satisfied. Lift that assemblage away to one side and lay over it a sheet of detail paper to keep things more or less in position.

Next, using a flat piece of card, paste a smooth layer of Cow Gum over the entire A4 area on the artwork. Working quickly, but not hastily, start pasting the elements, biggest first – main church logo, main headline – putting a smooth layer of Cow Gum on the back and sliding it onto the grid in its appropriate place before the gum sets. Take care not to spread the gum thickly and keep a piece of paper over the artwork up to the point you are currently working; when this piece gets sticky, discard it as you must not transfer gum to the face of the headline lettering or the typing. Working steadily in this way, you transfer the elements from your loose assembly sheet to the artwork. Leave illustrations till last, preferably with the photos untrimmed (if they are of a size to be pasted directly onto the artwork) and the drawings undrawn; this allows you a final flexibility.

Do not be afraid of the Cow Gum. A piece that does not go down square can be pushed into position and if it has set too hard for that, it can be peeled back up, regummed and done again; if it gets smudged, you can retype the paragraph and paste it directly over the offending part. Even days later, if done carefully, sections can be removed with the help of lighter fuel (Cow Gum's solvent). Last, paste down your illustrations.

Where a photo is over — or undersize and you have had to mask and scale it, simply leave in a pencil area on the layout, within which is a letter key to match the one written on the illustration's overlay; the printer will then put it in at plate-making stage. Clean off the Cow Gum using a Cow-rubber, holding a clean sheet of paper up to the edges of text elements so that you do not smear them. By positioning a desk lamp to throw light across the artwork towards you, the texture of the remaining gum will be perfectly visible. You will remove many of the pencil lines during this stage, and you can clean off any others with a putty rubber — all, that is, apart from the pencilled keymarks. These you must now ink-in with the Rapidograph, writing in at the same time the size instructions to the printer ('same size' or 'reduce to 210mm'). When the ink is dry, erase the pencil keymarks. Then repeat the process for the other page.

Cover each A4 printing area with an A4 sheet of detail paper, lightly taped along the top edge so that the printer can remove it without tearing the artwork surface. If you have positioned the two pages centrally you can fold the A2 cartridge sheet on which the artwork is pasted neatly in half, inwards. To make this fold neat, lay your steel rule along that central vertical space and run the blunt back of the scalpel down it, thus scoring but not cutting the paper. When folded in this way it can be slipped into a cardboard sleeve and protected from damage. Get the Writer to proofread the artwork before passing to the Fixer for printing.

Technical Information

The Designer naturally accumulates helpful references and samples of print materials over a period, as will the Fixer. At the start only a few are necessary. On any aspect of design, artwork or printing there is a plethora of published works, a good selection of which will be available at your local library. Unless you are ambitious to become more technically skilled than this role strictly demands, keep things simple.

International paper sizes (also known as ISO) are now becoming standard in Britain as well as Europe, only a few specialist or old-fashioned printers clinging on to traditional sizes – which always were a muddle. The sizing system is calculated to save paper and offers a range of sub-sizes and envelope compatibility. The technically-minded will be glad to know that it is based on a rectangle whose sides have a ratio of one to the square root of 2. This means that A2 is half the size of A1 and double the size of A3, and so on. There are three of these ISO series. Each is given an O suffix, and here we give two of these series only – AO, general printing sizes, and CO, envelope sizes, leaving out the BO series of poster sizes. For your purposes, getting the paper and envelope sizes matched is a first consideration.

Printers will always help by explaining how their machines can cope with paper sizes and folding. Not all of them will stock all the envelope sizes but will order them if you insist. There are simple folds: halved A4 (the usual size for letter-headings) makes A5 (many church magazines are basically A4s folded into A5s after photocopying or stencil-printing and

GENERAL PRINTING			ENVELOPES		
Sizes	Millimetres	Approx inches	Sizes	Millimetres	Approx inches
A0	841 x 1189	33⅛ x 46¾	C0	917 x 1297	36⅛ x 51
A1	594 x 841	23⅜ x 33⅛	C1	648 x 917	25½ x 36⅛
A2	420 x 594	16½ x 23⅜	C2	458 x 648	18 x 25½
A3	297 x 420	11¾ x 16½	C3	324 x 458	12¾ x 18
A4	210 x 297	8¼ x 11¾	C4	229 x 324	9 x 12¾
A5	148 x 210	5⅞ x 8¼	C5	162 x 229	6⅜ x 9
A6	105 x 148	4⅛ x 5⅞	C6	114 x 162	4½ x 6⅜
A7	74 x 105	2⅞ x 4⅛	C7	81 x 114	3¼ x 4½
A8	52 x 74	2 x 2⅞	C8	57 x 81	2¼ x 3¼
A9	37 x 52	1½ x 2	DL	110 x 220	4¾ x 8⅝
A10	26 x 37	1 x 1½	C7/6	81 x 162	3¼ x 6⅜

stapled into a preprinted cover); but many more complex folds are available. Thus 24-page brochures, for example, may be printed on a huge sheet of paper, folded several times and then trimmed before stapling; in such cases artwork preparation is tricky as the 'imposition' (the disposition of individual pages) demands some to be inverted and all to be arranged in an apparently illogical sequence. Even at your most ambitious, it is unlikely your budget will permit such elaboration, but as you become more experienced there are some neat folds you may have a chance to consider.

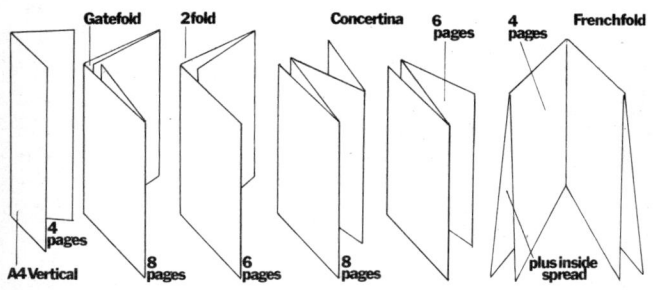

Conclusion

Beyond all the planning, beyond all the discussion about how to solve problems in church communication, beyond all the nuts and bolts of writing, reporting, and designing – there are people who do not know Christ. What I've tried to do in this book is to examine the ways and means of reaching those people inexpensively, effectively, and – I hope – with sincerity. *Message on a Shoestring* has by its nature concentrated on those ways and means rather than on the ultimate purposes behind them – which are the subject of many other books about theology in general and evangelism in particular. But in the end, if we lose sight of real people with real needs, we have not made messages at all; we have spoken into a void and remained locked in our own Christian ghetto. In the end, if our only reason for church growth promotions is to raise more money so that we can grow to larger numbers to raise more money . . . then we have done nothing at all to honour God and his Kingdom. In the end, too, if we haven't enjoyed making messages, then all we have communicated is our own lacklustre and lukewarm 'churchiness'; certainly no-one hears the Gospel.

It is my hope and prayer, then, that we shall be deeply enough convinced of our mission to those outside the Church to think creatively, to speak clearly, and to enjoy sharing our faith in Christ Jesus.

> *'Sir,' they said, 'from now on give us this bread.' Then Jesus declared, 'I am the bread of life. He who comes to me will never go hungry, and he who believes in me will never be thirsty.'*
>
> John 6:34–36
>
> *Chris Radley, 1986*

Index